FUTUREKIND
DESIGN
BY
AND
FOR
THE
PEOPLE
ROBERT PHILLIPS

FOREWORD BY
YVES BÉHAR

Over 500 illustrations

Futurekind

Thames & Hudson

Robert Phillips is a senior tutor on the Design Products + Futures Programme at the Royal College of Art, London. He is also a highly experienced product designer, having worked both independently and in the commercial sector. One of his most recent projects, My Naturewatch, a collaboration with the Interaction Research Studio at Goldsmiths, University of London, was featured on BBC's *Springwatch*.

Yves Béhar is a designer, entrepreneur and educator. He is the CEO of Fuseproject, the San Francisco-based design and branding firm he established in 1999, and has collaborated with such companies as Herman Miller, Samsung and Prada. Béhar's works are included in the permanent collections of museums worldwide, and he is a frequent speaker on design, sustainability and business subjects.

Futurekind: Design by and for the People
© 2019 Thames & Hudson Ltd, London

Text © 2019 Robert Phillips

Foreword © 2019 Yves Béhar

Taxonomic illustrations © 2019 James Tooze

Designed by Pete Rossi/RM&CO

First published in 2019 in the United States of America by Thames & Hudson Inc., 500 Fifth Avenue, New York, New York 10110

www.thamesandhudsonusa.com

Library of Congress Control Number 2018956113

ISBN 978-0-500-51979-0

Printed in China by RR Donnelley

+ FUTUREKIND
+ CONTENTS

Making is what will get us to a better world.

I was lucky: I grew up during the punk era. Being punk meant you could be an amateur at whatever you wanted to do, and use your own skills to make anything. And since the results didn't have to live up to traditional expectations around perfectly finished goods, it was easy for me to feel welcome and just start making. Using a sewing machine, spray paint and a basic saw or drill in my parents' basement, I made clothes, furniture and various items of my own invention. I quickly found myself surrounded by friends and other makers. We were a band of cartoonists, musicians, painters and fashion and graphic designers. We pushed one another's craft, without fear of failing or exposing the rough edges of our creations.

Futurekind reminds me of my own open-source and community-oriented youth in the design world. It is with certainty that I can say this: those early experiences encouraged me to pursue a life in design. I believe humanity needs more making, more design and more inventions. The question is, how do we encourage young makers to take a leap of faith? *Futurekind* shows us the way: makers from all around the world attempting to solve problems with the materials at their disposal. Human ingenuity in action. Humanity doing the hard work of trying to improve its lot, our community and our planet.

Nothing gives me greater hope and joy than simply watching others make, collaborate, and create new networks of support and distribution. And let's not forget: making is thinking in action. For too long we have separated design thinking from design making. I have argued for some time that, throughout history, the best makers have been the best thinkers. From Charles and Ray Eames to George Nelson, Bruno Munari, Achille Castiglioni and countless others, such designer-thinkers have provided us with the most beautiful objects and experiences, while expanding design theory and criticism.

Making and thinking are inherently related throughout *Futurekind*. Its pages are filled with the process of discovery and the intent of the projects' makers. The aims are clear: changing the world and finding solutions that industry or governments have failed to provide. What we see is the creative process multiplied by the accessibility of modern design tools – 3D printing, online platforms, artificial intelligence, all contributing to an age of design for the social good.

Futurekind shows us how open-source and community-focused designers are tackling some of the most urgent problems: by asking better questions and understanding needs, exploring possibilities, prototyping solutions, refining, failing and starting over. It's a cycle. A human cycle of creativity and design.

Yves Béhar
Founder and CEO, Fuseproject

Using this Book

On the opening page of each project, a series of illustrations identifies the project's architecture and key attributes. All the projects, while unique, have repeatable features, blueprints and foundations. The intention is for you, the reader, to use the information contained in the project descriptions and build on the experience of these highly successful design interventions. The definitions of the illustrations are provided opposite and overleaf.

USER-GENERATED
Content and outputs created
by anyone.

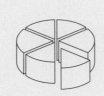

STAKEHOLDERS
People/organizations involved in
or affected by a design process,
output or intervention.

RESEARCH
Navigating unknown
factors to understand their
implications and discover
opportunities or challenges.

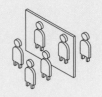

CULTURAL CHALLENGES
Challenges that have a
geographical, social or
religious element.

ECONOMIC ANALYSIS
Studying the production,
distribution and use of income,
wealth and commodities.

CHALLENGE IDENTIFICATION
Determining the benefits,
pitfalls and opportunities of
a situation or context.

TECHNOLOGY DEVELOPMENT
The application and development
of knowledge for practical ends.

INTELLECTUAL PROPERTY
Ownership of original creative
thought, as patents, copyrighted
material or trademarks.

CROWDFUNDED
A group or community contributing
finance to a common cause or
opportunity.

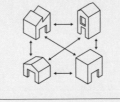

DISTRIBUTED MANUFACTURING
The production of goods using
a network of manufacturing
facilities in different locations.

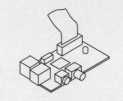

ACCESSIBLE TECHNOLOGIES
Tools and other enabling resources
that are available to all.

ACCESSIBLE DESIGN
Making design outcomes available
to everyone.

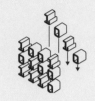

DATA CREATION
The generation of facts, statistics
and other items of information.

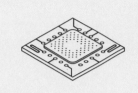

TECHNOLOGY
A tool that furthers the
capabilities of its users.

MASS MANUFACTURE
The large-scale
production of goods.

PUBLIC PARTICIPATION
People or communities having an
active role in a process/system.

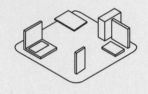

PLATFORM
Common elements (components,
parts or technologies) shared
across a range of products.

ECONOMIC SYSTEM
A system of production, resource
allocation and distribution of
goods and services within a society
or a given geographic area.

TRANSPARENCY
Business and financial activities
completed without secrets,
thereby building trust.

USER-DIRECTED
A process or outcome
guided by its participants.

DEMOCRATIZATION
Making something democratic
and accessible.

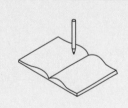

RESOURCE CREATION
The creation of products,
tools or knowledge for
use in future projects.

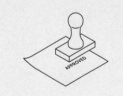

EXPERT VALIDATION
The consultation and approval
of expert parties.

VALUE-ADDING
Lending value to a process,
product or initiative.

EMPLOYMENT
The provision of work and
related economic benefits.

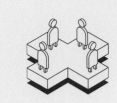

SOCIETAL BENEFIT
Having a positive impact
on the wider society.

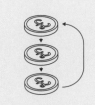

FINANCIAL SUSTAINABILITY
Systems for the continuous
renewal of financial opportunities.

DATA
Information to be examined,
informing personal or global
actions and their implications.

KNOWLEDGE
Information obtained by
experience or study, and
either held by an individual
or shared among groups.

EMPOWERMENT
Giving a group of people more
freedom or rights through
a design intervention.

ENVIRONMENTAL
Relating to the natural habitats
of people, animals and plants.

SUSTAINABILITY
Working to avoid the depletion
of natural resources in order to
maintain an ecological balance.

GOVERNMENTAL
Measures, policies and regulations
set by governments.

HEALTH
Concerning an individual's
physical or mental wellbeing.

ACCESS
The right or opportunity to use,
review or change something.

[01] Thomas Paine, *Rights of Man: Common Sense, and Other Political Writings*, new edn (Oxford: Oxford University Press, 2008).

[02] John Thackara, *How to Thrive in the Next Economy: Designing Tomorrow's World Today* (London: Thames & Hudson, 2017).

[03] Design Council, 'Sarah Weir OBE: Design Council's First Female CEO', www.designcouncil.org.uk/news-opinion/sarah-weir-obe-design-councils-first-female-ceo, accessed 4 October 2018.

[04] World Economic Forum, 'Annual Report 2017–2018', www3.weforum.org/docs/WEF_Annual_Report_2017-2018.pdf, accessed 4 October 2018.

[05] Rahis Saifi, 'Pokémon GO's Mental Health Benefits are Real', *Huffington Post*, www.huffingtonpost.com/rahis-saifi/pokemon-gos-mental-health_b_11204184.html?guccounter=1, accessed 4 October 2018.

[06] The Trussell Trust, 'UK Foodbank Use Continues to Rise', www.trusselltrust.org/2017/04/25/uk-foodbank-use-continues-rise/, accessed 4 October 2018.

What is Futurekind?

Design is a catalyst, uniting manufacturing and business, users and usability, with far-reaching consequences. For the projects included in this book, the pertinent issues are societal impact, community-led insights and contextually appropriate design. As far back as 1791, the political revolutionary Thomas Paine stated that 'my country is the world and my religion is to do good',[01] while the contemporary designer John Thackara has observed that 'the next economy concerns meeting daily-life needs in ways that enhance, rather than degrade, social and ecological assets.'[02] Meanwhile, Sarah Weir, the CEO of the Design Council, believes that 'design provides imaginative, thoughtful and workable solutions to [the] challenges [that] people and society are grappling with.'[03] In *Futurekind*, a range of design, political and economic considerations combine with the needs of society, design forethought and collaboration, enabling a sustainable future.

Futurekind design is considerate of its social, local, global, human and material effects, which can often be hidden from view. The featured projects range from products and services to systems, building on both design-led and economic approaches. The lessons learned from these projects can be globally translated across cultures, contexts and different challenges.

The people helping to shape Futurekind are policy-makers, entrepreneurs, designers, social scientists, engineers, communicators, collaborators, architects and, hopefully, you. We believe that everyone should be able to engage with the issues that directly affect them, their communities and/or their surroundings. One solution is simply to design communally, 'for a better world, by being socially distributed, engaged and accessible'. The collaborative examples discussed in these pages unify expertise and communities, rather than 'parachuting in' established values.

We don't intend to preach, as we do not know the answers; instead, we hope to learn and build on others' responses and approaches to global challenges. Such issues require collaboration in order to navigate, unpick and address them fully, engaging economics, business models, capacity, government, social sciences, legal constraints, human rights, cultural knowledge and more. The projects considered here encourage people to access the resources they need, drawing on their own invaluable insights and experience. We are in an age of the 'enablers' of Futurekind, empowering people to build, re-appropriate and distribute ideas:

enablers +
communities +
agency +
capability =
opportunities

Why should we become Futurekind?

According to the World Economic Forum, the key issues facing humanity include extreme weather events, cyberattacks, natural disasters, ageing populations, the increasing polarization of society, climate change, terrorism and food and water shortages. In its annual report of 2017–18, it claimed that '90% of people live with polluted air'; children are increasingly likely to live in a 'degrading environment'; and growing numbers of people 'will live in urban areas resulting in sprawling cities'.[04]

We are living in an age of change. Digitally well connected, we are also more isolated than ever, with such gaming platforms as Pokémon GO providing surprising solutions to mental-health problems.[05] As the world becomes 'Uberized' and more connected, products are transforming. A report by the Trussell Trust published in 2017 found that food-bank usage was on the rise, 'providing 1,182,954 emergency food supplies to people in crisis compared to 1,109,309 in 2015–16'.[06] The waste we produce has a long tail, affecting the environment and wildlife, with BBC's *Blue Planet* bringing the plastic-waste crisis into our living rooms. According to the McKinsey Center for Business and Environment, 'five trillion … pieces of microplastic are in the ocean, with one rubbish truck load added each minute.'[07] The impact on ourselves and our world will take generations to comprehend and counter.

In 2016 a report by the Royal Society for the Protection of Birds highlighted that '15% of species in Great Britain are thought to be extinct or threatened with extinction'.[08] Governments are waging war on childhood

[07] McKinsey Center for Business and Environment, 'Stemming the Tide: Land-based Strategies for a Plastic-free Ocean', www.mckinsey.com/~/media/mckinsey/business%20functions/sustainability%20and%20resource%20productivity/our%20insights/stemming%20the%20tide/stemming%20the%20tide%20land%20based%20strategies%20for%20a%20plastic%20free%20ocean.ashx, accessed 4 October 2018.

[08] Royal Society for the Protection of Birds, 'State of Nature 2016', www.rspb.org.uk/globalassets/downloads/documents/conservation-projects/state-of-nature/state-of-nature-uk-report-2016.pdf, accessed 4 October 2018.

[09] HM Revenue & Customs, 'Soft Drinks Industry Levy' (policy paper), www.gov.uk/government/publications/soft-drinks-industry-levy/soft-drinks-industry-levy, accessed 4 October 2018.

[10] World Economic Forum, 'The Global Risks Report 2016' (11th edition), www.zurichsigorta.com.tr/uploads/risk-report/file/2016.pdf?=a2b056c52b8a4e38ab5bf8ed34d1a3d1, accessed 4 October 2018.

[11] See zooniverse.org, accessed 4 October 2018.

obesity with 'sugar taxes', hoping to curb our addictions.[09] Water scarcity is rocketing, with the charity Save the Water predicting an impact on communities, farming, political stability and even peace in years to come.[10] Crucially, these and other global challenges are interrelated, requiring holistic, socially motivated responses.

How is Futurekind enabled?
Knowledge and expertise are being democratized through 'enablers', attainable processes, platforms or systems used by communities to achieve their aspirations. Zooniverse's 'people-powered research', for example, has rapidly transformed citizens' participation in global scientific challenges.[11] Communication tools are commonplace, with social-media plug-ins, platforms and wikis consolidating knowledge. In computing, such open-source hardware as Arduino, Raspberry Pi and BBC micro:bit, as well as coding clubs for children, are transforming skill sets. Using digital files shared over the internet, CNC machines and 3D printers can produce goods locally, eliminating the need for international shipping. This democratization of tools leads to a 'perfect storm' of agency, with communities engaging directly with the issues that most concern them. Lead users are designing with and for communities in 'maker spaces', including fab labs (fabrication laboratories) and open workshops.

Access to finance has also been transformed, with entrepreneurship programmes, crowdfunding and other online platforms operating on the basis of the quality of ideas, rather than age, gender, culture or experience. The potential for unskilled communities to use maker spaces to create their own tools, design equipment and improve their lives is compelling. These movements have not yet unseated professional practitioners, however, not least because the process of democratizing or opening up design is more complicated than just placing blueprints on the internet. The legal requirements, quality standards, technical skills and political know-how required to design and manufacture a product are exceedingly complex; unskilled parents making children's toys from online plans, for example, could result in the creation of choking hazards. Nevertheless, we are already used

to a certain amount of 'local manufacture' at appropriate skill levels – self-assembly toys, flat-pack furniture, kit cars, home DIY.

The physical and digital tools discussed above are giving people access not only to things they can make, but also to the means to manipulate designs. This mixed-capability economy enables people to develop personal 'tech for good', governing, sharing, distributing or turning a profit from their 'accessible designs'. My own experience of an 'enablers + communities + agency' scenario occurred during my PhD research trial, helping beekeepers to construct their own technologies to investigate their colonies. The research highlighted the desire that grassroots communities have for positively understanding their environment. There are now numerous initiatives in which disparate, unfunded groups are using data that they've gathered to lobby government and legislative bodies.

Where should we be Futurekind?
Futurekind should not be limited to economically challenged areas, but should be making things better for all – creating appropriate design interventions, listening to global needs. Design practice is not a one-dimensional pursuit; it involves sustainability issues (economic and environmental), communications, stakeholders and the crossing of multiple boundaries. Collectively, we should be tackling the larger issues at hand, addressing the lack of civic empowerment and agency. Ideas for bringing about change are widely available in the form of accessible design that can be downloaded. Access to knowledge can be used to create economic empowerment, and community engagement to provide economic stability. Finally, we should foster collaborative communities, generating environmental sustainability that, in turn, builds positive behaviour, health and wellbeing.

When should we become Futurekind?
With access to a swathe of new technologies, our generation has a historic opportunity to make a difference. But it is not without its challenges. It is hoped that the projects that make up this book will inspire humankind to act *now*, making Futurekind a reality.

+

001
CIVIC
EMPOW

001
CIVIC EMPOWERMENT

ER
MENT

FUTURE SENSE

Building agency through sensor technology

+ 001CE/FS/01

+ 001CE/FS/02

The Future Sense project was conceived to explore how emerging low-cost sensor technology (001CE/FS/02), combined with increased internet access, could add value to social enterprises. Although the final prototypes focused on agriculture, the team experimented with ideas in energy, safety, health, and sanitation.. Initial products include a moisture sensor that gives farmers an overview of water levels, and GPS land-mapping equipment. The solar-powered moisture sensor indicates excess, inadequate or optimal ground moisture. The data gathered helps agents analyse farmland, assessing soil types, drainage rates and weather patterns. The data is reciprocal for arranging farm loans, reducing the risks faced by farmers and funders. In an interview, IDEO.org's design director Adam Reineck shared his insights.

IDEO.org had three years of innovation funding from the Wasserman Fund and Autodesk Foundation to work with organizations that push the boundaries of innovation and technology in the social sector. They 'used the funding on a variety of projects, including a more exploratory strategy on drones for last-mile health delivery'. Reineck said '[the] work opened our eyes to the importance of exploring opportunities that emerging tech might play a role in across the social sector, a space that generally lacks investment in design-led, human-centred

innovation. After the drones' work, we began vetting other emerging technologies that could have a huge impact on the lives of the poor, and narrowed to precision agriculture as one big area (001CE/FS/03). Sensor tech is suddenly cheaper, more available and easier to prototype with than ever, and people have increasing access to phones, smartphones and connectivity in many of the poorest countries, representing opportunities to leapfrog and make big innovations happen quickly.'

They started by interviewing agriculture organizations and sensor tech companies to understand the stage the tech was at, and learn what the biggest needs were in international smallholder agriculture (001CE/FS/04). Reineck said they had also 'worked on a wide variety of agriculture projects here, touching product, service, brand, and strategy, and used that experience to do initial research in Kenya, Tanzania, and Myanmar to understand the needs at a deeper level and prototype potential solutions'.

Throughout their work they see smallholder farmers struggling to maintain sustainable livelihoods; as Reineck said, 'many people are leaving their farms, and those that stay are increasingly prone to the effects of climate change. We believe that, by enabling farmers

+ + As practitioners of human-centred design, we always believe in starting with understanding the people who might be using what we're designing – although when it comes to future technologies that don't currently exist, this process requires prototyping.

+ 001CE/FS/03

+ 001CE/FS/04

+ 020

+ FUTUREKIND
+ 001 CIVIC EMPOWERMENT

+ FUTURE SENSE

OPPOSITE:
+ 001CE/FS/06

+ + Sensor tech is suddenly cheaper, more available, and easier to prototype with than ever, and people have increasing access to phones, smartphones and connectivity in many of the poorest countries, representing opportunities to leapfrog and make big innovations happen very quickly.

+ 001CE/FS/05

to receive better feedback on the farm (weather data, understanding what's going on beneath the soil surface, applying inputs more effectively, etc.), we can move to a more efficient and profitable model that changes the current narrative of farming development. The model that is spread around most of the world goes back to the green revolution in the 1950s, prioritizing consolidation of small farms, monocultures, heavy fertilizer and pesticide use. This is fundamentally not a sustainable direction. Smallholder farmers can thrive by embracing better practices and new technologies.'

During a field trial of moisture-sensor prototypes, one of the project partners, Proximity Designs, found that 80% of farmers were over-irrigating their fields, on average by 28%, leading to problems including fungus and other diseases, and lower yields. They sold eight low-res soil moisture sensors and returned two months later to learn about five farmers' experiences. They found that, in general, the farmers had reduced irrigation by 25–30%. Two out of the five reported less fungus on their onion crops, while all of them reported saving around 30% in fuel costs (700–1,000 kyats per month). Reineck shared their key insights: '[Future Sense] started by looking very broadly at

the needs and opportunities that come up continually in our work, and exploring how emerging sensor tech could potentially create impact in those areas through research and prototyping. This process involves a lot of rigour and focus to avoid becoming lost in ambiguity. We balanced this by engaging in user research, interviewing experts, building to think (prototyping ideas) and other methods that helped us narrow to focused solutions. There is huge value in this forward-thinking exploratory work in the social impact space, because the non-profit sector is largely focused on the problems of today, and solves challenges by looking at past data and proven methods over looking to emerging tech and trends.' As practitioners of human-centred design, he said, 'we always believe in starting with understanding the people who might be using what we're designing – although when it comes to future technologies that don't currently exist, this process requires prototyping a lot of potential solutions and finding ways for people to interact with them from day one. As long as we are unattached to the things we're building, we iterate and follow the path to working solutions. This is an emergent area in human-centred design that works well for future visions.'

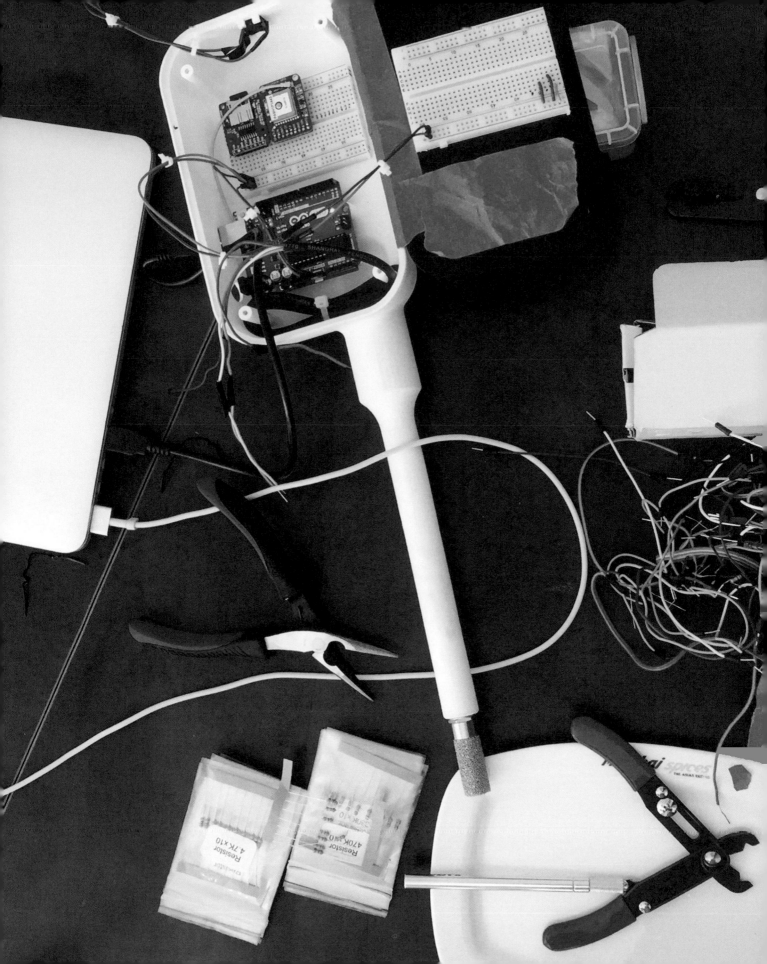

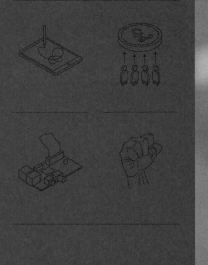

FIX MY STREET

Community empowerment through onsite reporting

+ 001CE/FMS/02

FixMyStreet is a simple way to report street problems in communities, with participants reporting problems such as potholes, unsafe pavements and broken streetlights. It is a map-based interface, matching geographical points to email addresses (001CE/FMS/01). The concept for FixMyStreet arose when the founder of mySociety, Tom Steinberg, found himself walking past a vandalized phone box on a daily basis. He realized that he didn't know who to report it to – and that, while most citizens would be quite willing to report such local community issues, most would not know exactly how to do so. mySociety found that there is confusion around common street problems; the two-tier council system in the UK means that while people may be aware that these should be reported to 'the council', they do not always know which one.

Trying to report something often involves visiting one or more council websites to ascertain responsibility, then finding the reporting functionality on an internal page, then wading through pages of forms designed with the council's needs in mind, rather than usability. FixMyStreet covers the whole of the UK, so you can make a report even if you are not in your local area, at www.fixmystreet. com. It collects the minimum amount of data possible in order to make an efficient, actionable report to the council, which makes it quick and intuitive to use. There is one other important facet of FixMyStreet, which comes from mySociety's focus on transparency and accountability: FixMyStreet publishes reports and responses online. It builds a public picture of the main neighbourhood issues, and local authority responses. They've heard anecdotally that, when issues are published online, councils have been quicker to act.

FixMyStreet works equally well in urban or rural areas, and can be used by anyone with an internet connection. Importantly, the FixMyStreet software is open source, meaning people can modify it and use it for their own purposes; this has led to FixMyStreet sites in 19 countries worldwide, from South America to Australia. The software, a mechanism matching geographical points with bodies responsible for reports, has been used for other purposes, including reporting empty homes (in partnership with Channel 4), cataloguing antisocial behaviour on public transport, and documenting cycling collisions. Impact is measured through one particular metric, asking every user of FixMyStreet whether they have ever contacted their local government before in any way. Since FixMyStreet's launch in 2007, this figure has always been above 50%, which indicates that the site is empowering people who had not previously thought of 'owning' local problems.

FixMyStreet were asked: how should we design for social change? They cited the fast-moving nature of the internet, meaning that they have to constantly adapt. A recent example of this is the increased use of mobile phones for internet access over the past few years: FixMyStreet's launch pre-dated that shift, so there was work to do when it became clear that people wanted to report issues while out and about. Of course, it makes perfect sense now. Over the past couple of years FixMyStreet has added GPS reporting, responsive design, apps for iOS and Android, and a behaviour flow that works slightly differently on mobile. Its open-source nature allows it to accept code modifications made by contributors all over the world.

When questioned about the lessons they can learn from, FixMyStreet responded: 'No matter how many barriers we break down and no matter how easy design makes it for everyone to engage with their elected representatives, there will always be some people who feel less able to do so. One major issue that design can't tackle on its own, but can still play an integral part in, is how to make everyone feel that they bear equal responsibility for their community and that they have the power to get things changed.'

FixMyStreet is a straightforward model whereby citizens can demand that broken things get fixed. But mySociety also provide websites that allow citizens to keep track of parliamentary goings-on, contact their MPs and, where suitable, make freedom of information requests. They said that '[in] all of these, the challenge is the same – how do you make people feel that they are responsible, and not just leave this kind of monitoring to the ones who have historically shouted the loudest? Friendly, accessible, undemanding interface design ensures everyone participates in their democracy.'

SOLAR
STOVE

Using abundant
resources to build
better products
internationally

+ + In the beginning, we focused on a handful of rural villages in the Himalayas. Now, we have customers in over 60 countries around the world.

+ 001CE/SS/02

+ 001CE/SS/03

Dr Catlin Powers, co-founder of One Earth Designs – the organization behind the SolSource solar stove – was inspired by a Himalayan research trip, on which she encountered a nomadic Tibetan community. They demonstrated their indoor stove pollution, presenting an air-quality challenge. When measured, the air quality was ten times more polluted than the air in Beijing. The World Health Organization states that four million people die every year from breathing 'stove smoke', more than die from AIDS and malaria combined. The nomads faced fuel scarcity, making alternative fuel options a priority. A five-year collaboration yielded 54 different solar-powered prototypes, finally arriving at SolSource. It heats up five times faster than a charcoal grill, delivering 1,000 watts of power, and harnesses sunlight seven times more efficiently than an average photovoltaic solar panel. SolSource's mission is to help people live sustainably within 'one earth' resources, for those seeking affordable, clean-energy cooking (001CE/SS/01).

One Earth Designs' customers include off-grid families and people concerned with the financial, health and ecological implications of cooking fuel (001CE/SS/02). SolSource is a clean solar cooking alternative that saves lives and money, and opens up various opportunities. SolSource has reduced smoke pollution in customers' homes by a factor of five, saving over 500,000 working days for women – time that they would otherwise have spent collecting fuel. The organization has won countless awards, including the EPA's People, Prosperity & the Planet Award, the MIT IDEAS

Award (three years in a row) and many more. A village leader suggested using the sun to address the massive fuel scarcity issue faced by his community. In the rural Himalayas, SolSource lowers carbon emissions and fuel consumption, saves time for women, saves money, and reduces smoke exposure from indoor stoves.

Annually, each person using SolSource reduces their pollution exposure by the equivalent of 4,300 cigarettes. One of the project attributes is the 'better for all' international approach, with celebrity chefs queuing up to experiment with the stoves. The designers of SolSource believe that 'social design and social technology use the tools of design and technology to benefit humanity. Life on Earth will sustain with or without humans. Whether Earth remains a good home for humans, however, is dependent on the decisions we make and the actions we take on a daily basis. At One Earth Designs we use design and technology tools to help people live well and prosper within the resource capacity of our planet.'

When interviewed, One Earth Designs responded with an important repeatable lesson for this type of work: 'Listen and build value.' They say that pioneering a new innovation or building a company, especially in areas with little business infrastructure, requires you to be fully present and to take care of yourself. With this in mind: 'First, make sure that being fully present with your venture is what you really want. If so, then structure your life for resilience. You must be emotionally, physically and psychologically prepared to face challenges

+ 026

+ FUTUREKIND
+ 001 CIVIC EMPOWERMENT

+ SOLAR STOVE

OPPOSITE:
+ 001CE/SS/04

that push you beyond your boundaries, time and time again. When the world knocks you down, you must be prepared to get up smiling and try again – this time smarter, better, faster. Usually, this is easier when you are healthy, well rested and have people who will be there for you when the going gets rough.'

To One Earth Designs, 'listen and build value' means that success lies in creating value that your customers and partners care about. 'Build listening into the structure of your business so that you continue to evolve your understanding of how to create meaningful value for the people you serve. Don't forget to build value for the partners you work with to deliver value to your customers, too. Without them, you cannot succeed. Similarly, social entrepreneurs often focus on their end customer and forget to create value throughout the supply chain. Building listening into the structure of your business enables you to continuously evolve your understanding of how to create meaningful value for the people you serve. Specifically, incorporating local business norms, currencies (including bartering) and an understanding of your customers' and partners' motivations can make the difference between success and failure.'

Sometimes, they said, 'we forget to step back and look at the macro perspective. Take time to put your work in perspective on an ongoing basis. It will improve your strategies and help you choose wisely, to know when to accept the way things are and when to fight for the changes you care about (whether small or large).' In emerging markets, the organization relies on 'word of mouth and public demonstrations to achieve traction. One of our most successful techniques is offering customers a small commission for sales they make within their village, and a slightly higher rate for sales made outside their village.' They said that social technology 'can become more financially sustainable by aiming to create value that your customers and partners care about and are willing to pay for. Many social entrepreneurs forget that value is in the eye of the beholder. If your customers don't already see why your product is worth buying, ask yourself, why not? If your product isn't actually creating value, how can you change it so that it does? If it is creating value but people don't realize it, how do you educate your customers?' Finally, they say we should not 'expect to get things right. In a world where the only constant is change, the only strategy for success is constant learning.'

+ + The World Health Organization states that four million people die every year from breathing 'stove smoke'; that is more than die from AIDS and malaria combined.

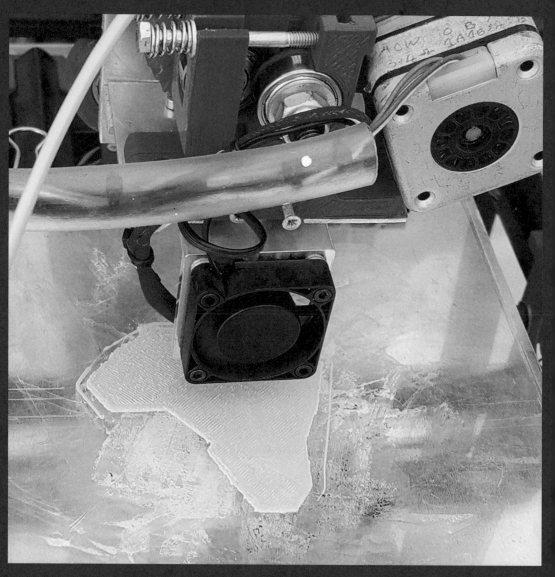

+ 001CE/TFT/01

TECH FOR TRADE

Technology that leverages commerce, enabling local change

+ + Learn by doing, putting the product into the hands of the users and finding out what happens when you do that, as quickly as possible.

+ 001CE/TFT/02

TechforTrade is making 3D printing internationally affordable for all, by developing software (Retr3d) and taking e-waste components to build 3D printers (001CE/TFT/01). The technology is freely accessible online, for international use or appropriation. TechforTrade is the leading UK charity specifically focused on bridging the divide between emerging technology and international trade and economic development. It believes that many of the world's poorest communities are prevented from engaging effectively in trade and building their prosperity by fundamental market gaps or breakdowns in value chains. TechforTrade works at the interface of technology, trade and enterprise, with local entrepreneurs testing innovative approaches for sustainable and replicable businesses using technology to facilitate trade and alleviate poverty (001CE/TFT/06).

William Hoyle, CEO, founded TechforTrade after witnessing trucks crossing country borders and seeing 3D printing's potential to decrease import dependency. He started the 3D4D Challenge to encourage people to find meaningful uses for 3D printing; eventually, the development of 3D printing technologies became the charity's key focus. Their open-source software Retr3d helps users build custom 3D printers from such sources of e-waste as old inkjet printers and photocopiers, even including small fans to cool the machine. Retr3d calibrates the 3D printer and gets it to function. In this way, TechforTrade reduces the cost of 3D printer construction to between $100 and $120 per unit. It also created an 'ethical filament extruder' machine, costing

under $1,000, which recycles polyethylene terephthalate (PET – used in plastic bottle manufacture) into reels of 3D printer filament, at economical costs (001CE/TFT/07).

In an interview, Hoyle offered his insights. 'There is large potential to create small, community-based "digital blacksmiths" (001CE/TFT/04) – small businesses in places like Nairobi to make useful things for communities, such as educational aids, water and sanitation devices, medical devices or toys, as well as offering 3D printer services to the community, which they eventually receive payments for … Our hope is that we'll produce a blueprint for how these businesses can operate in a sustainable way, eventually creating a network of social enterprises working to use 3D printing to solve international problems.' He went on to say that the 'digital blacksmiths identified initiatives looking to leverage 3D printing technology for social impact in developing markets. We developed a manifesto for 3D printing technology as a transformative technology in the context of manufacturing.'

The charity's mission ensures that trade opportunities improve livelihoods and are open to the world's poorest people. The idea is to develop business concepts and models around new ideas, bringing fresh thinking to old problems. For example, it works in agriculture, developing trading platforms using data gathered from small agricultural traders to provide credit histories. 'That action enables banks to consider informal traders that don't keep records as being bankable.' That capability

+ + Design for the environment in which you are operating.

+ 001CE/TFT/03

+ 001CE/TFT/04

+ 001CE/TFT/05

+ 001CE/TFT/06

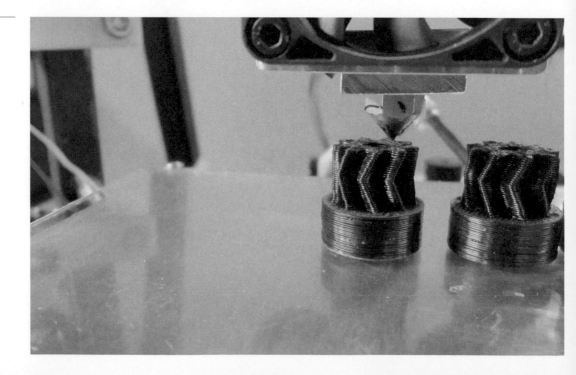

+ + TechforTrade ensures that trade opportunities improve livelihoods and are open to the world's poorest people.

+ 001CE/TFT/07

in turn increases access to working capital and the ability to build businesses, increasing their ability to produce more through local farmers to trade with buyers. 'That creates a new paradigm around bottom-up manufacturing, providing access to local products and developing new economy skills, around digital manufacturing.'

TechforTrade's strongest impact, they said, has been facilitating the waterscope, a low-cost microscope, fabricated in situ in Kenya or Tanzania. It is designed for numerous scenarios and environments, including education and veterinary and human health. Created to be biked to farm visits in places like rural Kenya, it has been used for the saliva testing of cattle, speeding up disease diagnosis of cattle herds. 'Designed appropriately for the market,' said Hoyle, 'it can be fixed if it breaks and comes in at about a third of the price of an equivalent imported model, while having exactly the same functionality. We have created a "poster child" for a high-value, high-impact product that can be made by a digital blacksmith, a digital artisan in a developing market, that addresses a real need, increasing the capability of agro-vets in rural areas.'

TechforTrade want to exemplify the model, evolving the dialogue on from 'Isn't this technology released to make mobile phone cases?' to providing concrete examples of things that can be done that are of high value and have high impact. They said they were 'really interested in developing minimal viable product testing on the ground, iterating the design of products'. They advised that if you

are designing for development and designing for impact in development, you should 'focus as quickly as you can on something that you think is a minimum viable product. Do it with the users in mind and get it out and test it quickly.' The idea, according to TechforTrade, is to 'literally learn by doing, putting the product into users hands and finding results when you do that, as quickly as possible'. Their main teaching point is to 'always design for the environment in which you are operating', while addressing the larger economics of building communities by designing 'appropriately'.

ON
OUR
RADAR

Community reporting
platform, for accurate
local stories

+ + On Our Radar's core mission is establishing an inclusive society where everyone is heard on the matters that affect them most, and can contribute to solutions.

+ 001CE/OOR/02

+ 001CE/OOR/03

On Our Radar is a non-profit communications agency focusing on under-reported stories from marginalized communities. In partnership with citizen journalists, one venture, 'Back in touch', helped locals reflect on life in Sierra Leone after Ebola (001CE/OOR/02). Their process relies on community reporting that is different from current citizen journalism models (001CE/OOR/03). They train networks trusted by local partners, with reporters nominated by their communities. The training teaches people how to report safely, verify facts, deal with sources, find stories, and so on. Post-submission, reporters' stories and outputs are verified for accuracy. As the immediacy of the Ebola crisis dissipated, On Our Radar found its storytelling partners told more human stories about love, loss, work and life beyond fatalities. This led to 'Back in touch', stories of people finding love and tackling loss after Ebola (001CE/OOR/01). Their method has produced broadcasts for Channel 4 News, resulting in millions of viewers. The system has built associations between councils and remote villages, connected media with communities in crisis and provided community-led insights. In interview, founder Libby Powell shared their design perspective.

A friendship with a dynamic photojournalist, who was tragically shot and killed in Gaza, inspired Powell to go beyond pure journalism. She said that an opportunity came up for her to join Medical Aid for Palestinians: 'I spent five years going between London and Lebanon, the Gaza Strip, the West Bank, talking with communities. While [I was] there, the war in Gaza happened.

The most powerful things we did were capture human stories, which remained untold. I entered a Guardian competition on international development, and ended up flying to Sierra Leone with a press pass to talk about disability. I was ferried around by NGOs and community groups, hearing positive stories of what young people with disabilities could do. I felt people with disabilities in Sierra Leone were being ignored, neglected, marginalized, and broke away to tell their stories. I produced a piece, full of anger at the way people are being treated, winning the competition and opening numerous doors. However, none of the journalistic work focused on human-centric processes or feedback to communities. I endeavoured to bring the best practices in international development and community empowerment through journalism, a value-driven journalistic practice, resulting in On Our Radar.'

On Our Radar's core mission, she said, is establishing an 'inclusive society where everyone is heard on the matters that affect them most and can contribute to solutions'. One of its numerous impacts included 'a young man called Seri Bangora, who was at our first training in Freetown. He is a crutch user, so he came in early to make himself comfortable. He ended up being one of our most active reporters. He used a mobile phone; he'd never been online before. He was a proud young man but hadn't been heard much outside of the disability rights movement. He reported on a massive democratic moment for his country using text messages, as his only means

+ 034

+ FUTUREKIND
+ 001 CIVIC EMPOWERMENT

+ ON OUR RADAR

OPPOSITE:
+ 001CE/OOR/05

+ 001CE/OOR/04

of communicating with us. As a result, he ended up working for us as a paid trainer.' When the Ebola outbreak hit, the team was in Freetown amid the health crisis. 'They sent quotes by text message and recorded voicemails. They painted this incredible picture of the outbreak as it was happening, but well beyond the spaces where the cameras could reach, behind the quarantine lines. After the outbreak, [Seri Bangora] helped to provide stories for the BBC and for Al Jazeera, and for Channel 4 (001CE/OOR/04). After the outbreak had dissipated, he trained a group of girls who were unable to return to education, helping them to tell their story. He has now established an organization using ISMS technology to help young people with disabilities report problems to the police.'

Powell said, 'If you are creative and you think fast, it's really easy to come up with incredible creative solutions using technology or social design to solve issues. Unless you have direct experience of that issue, you rarely fully understand the problem behind it. Due to projects that have almost failed, the only true way to design solutions is to understand the problem, through the eyes of those most affected. That doesn't mean tokenism; it means the solution request comes from them, or a well-timed piece of scoping work, enabling the users to lead the design. I suggest that people undertake a role as facilitators, more than tech practitioners or innovators.'

+ + After the Ebola outbreak had dissipated [Seri Bangora] trained a group of girls who were unable to return to education, helping them to tell their story. On Our Radar participants reported on the Ebola outbreak, a massive democratic moment for their country, using text messages as the only means of communicating with us.

+ 001CE/BS/01

Improving lives by
refining design

BETTER
SHELTER

+ + There are stories where people say that they can finally close a door behind them and just be within four walls; that's what we're here for.

+ 001CE/BS/02

+ 001CE/BS/03

Better Shelter is a social enterprise that develops and provides innovative housing solutions (001CE/BS/01). Their mission is to improve the lives of people displaced by conflicts and natural disasters, aiming 'to be the leader in emergency and temporary shelter innovation'. They want 'to be at the forefront, and never see the shelter as finished; [we] will always evolve'. Better Shelter was designed independently, and is a partnership between Better Shelter, the UN Refugee Agency (UNHCR) and the IKEA Foundation. The project's aim is to complement traditional refugee tents, as used in emergencies, with shelters designed for the post-emergency phase, which are more spacious (with higher ceilings), better insulated (clad in polypropylene panels) and more durable (lasting three years in moderate climates) than their counterparts. They have a galvanized-steel frame, polyolefin roof and wall panels, a locking door and solar-powered lamp, offering safety and security in scenarios that are anything but. Any profits made are reinvested within the company and will be used to further improve Better Shelter's solutions. The shelters' flat-pack design enables delivery and for them to be assembled by four people in roughly four to eight hours. Better Shelter has already made a big impact, with over 25,000 shelters deployed from Djibouti to Nepal (001CE/BS/02).

Better Shelters have been used in Djibouti, Ethiopia, Tanzania, Burundi, Rwanda, Niger, South Sudan, Mozambique, Senegal, Italy, Greece, Iraq, Fyr of Macedonia, Nepal, Bangladesh, Peru and Brazil. In interview, Märta Aretakis Terne, head of communications,

offered her insights. '[It is] important to state, we are not an IKEA product. It started as a design project at a "design foundation", in a small town in Sweden called Hällefors, where a group of students reviewed sustainable design. They started looking at tents, and quickly reviewed refugee camps, because, who lives in tents other than campers? From a lay perspective, they asked themselves, "Why do people still live in tents, the way they did 100 years ago after the earthquake in California?"'

The project formed 'between UNHCR and design colleagues, with funding from the IKEA Foundation. UNHCR provided requirements [for the shelters] to weigh under 100kg, cost below $1,000, and so on. They wanted [them] to be modular, have a door, a solar-powered lamp and features that tents did not have.' With the first prototypes, 'a number of refugee families moved into the shelters, to provide feedback. They also had a team of anthropologists studying the shelter use; what worked, what didn't. They tested them in three different climates, different cultures, etc., to get a wide array of feedback, with different-sized families.' Based on this feedback, Better Shelter worked on the design over two more years to arrive at industrialized versions.

Aretakis Terne said they were 'intended as temporary homes to begin with, but have been appropriated as clinics, child-friendly spaces, registration centres, staff accommodation, staff offices and more. For example, several hundreds of thousands of people travelled through Lesbos during 2015 and 2016, and we had 200

OPPOSITE:
+ 001CE/BS/04

+ FUTUREKIND
+ 001 CIVIC EMPOWERMENT

+ BETTER SHELTER

+ 039

+ 001CE/BS/05

+ 001CE/BS/06

shelters there. Families stayed for a few nights, so we've had hundreds of thousands of people staying in them, which is amazing. The lamps and PV [photovoltaic] systems disappeared from every shelter after one night, because you take whatever you can use on the road (001CE/BS/04). We're still evaluating their use, and what's not working.' She said the organization had had numerous impacts, 'especially in Iraq; people [have said] it feels like the first time they can embrace coming home after fleeing their homes. Our shelter is deployed in the post-emergency phase. But as you know, tents tend to be the solution that people remain in for several years. There are stories where people say they can finally close a door behind them and just be within four walls (001CE/BS/05).'

When questioned about lessons learned, Aretakis Terne responded: 'Things require change, but what we've witnessed and heard from professionals is, avoid neophilia – avoid trying to do something completely new – because it's impossible. It's hard to introduce that to such a large market where things move slowly and where low-tech solutions are still the most widely used (001CE/BS/06).' She also said that being naïve has helped. 'Being open, not knowing everything that we probably had to know to be able to develop something

for this industry, has helped because you continue trying, because you don't know all your obstacles. If we had known how hard this would be, I don't know if anyone would have done it.' Finally, she said, 'do it for the right reasons. That's the same reason we're all in the office after hours and working our arses off: because we care. We're all paid, it's a job that matters. It's good to be idealistic. Not everyone in the company has to be, but you need a few people who keep on going ... because they care with their hearts.'

+ + Any profits made are reinvested within the company and will be used to further improve Better Shelter's solutions.

Better access, with
crowdsourced upkeep
and maintenance

OPEN
TOILETS

+ 001CE/OT/02

+ 001CE/OT/03

Public toilets are not often considered a 'piece of design', though we all use them: for ourselves and our families, changing our babies, and providing dignity and security. 'Publicly accessible toilets' refers to all toilets that the public can access without purchasing anything, including in shopping centres, parks and transport hubs. Accessing and using a toilet while away from home is a serious issue in public life. Toilets are plagued by misuse; they are overwhelmed by bad design; parents do not wish to leave their children unattended, presenting a constant challenge. A report by Help the Aged found that 80% of respondents had difficulty in locating a public toilet, 78% found public toilets not open when required, and over half (52%) agreed that a lack of provision prevented them from going out. There are socio-cultural factors preventing discourse around accessible toilets, as many find the subject distasteful or embarrassing. With this in mind, the Great British Public Toilet Map, created by the Helen Hamlyn Centre for Design at the Royal College of Art, shows publicly accessible toilets (001CE/OT/01). The data comes from councils, businesses, OpenStreetMap and participants. The project encourages local councils to share data, accessible by smartphones and online tools. Dr Jo-Anne Bichard, project co-founder, shared her insights in an interview.

The project's mission, she said, was 'to provide information on publicly accessible toilets to the users who need them'. They conducted research with users, specialists, architects, people who commission toilets, people who clean toilets, and people who manage toilets. 'There was a discrepancy in the information people had about provision, presenting a design challenge. There's a big tension between toilet providers and toilet users. Users want more toilets, and providers want to ensure users don't do anything other than go to the toilet in them.' The project's initiation 'coincided with the emergence of open data as major information. We got open data on some toilets and provided digital notifications on where they were, creating a two-way communication channel.' It was social technological access to information that propelled the Great British Public Toilet Map; a 'community-involved venture, getting local authorities to support the government call, of

creating open data. Some councils have literally mapped every lamppost in the country. But they didn't know where toilets were, presenting a need. The London Olympics liked the idea. But when the map was eventually released it was very London-centric, and we did get criticism for that.' Now, with additional funding, Bichard said, 'we asked every UK local authority ... to give us their open data on toilets. And many of them helped populate the Toilet Map; we now have over 10,000 toilets listed in the UK. We are the most comprehensive database of "publicly accessible toilet provision", which is not only public toilets, but also toilets operated by providers such as National Rail, because believe it or not, they are a private provider.'

The project's greatest impact has been in relation to patient support services, especially for people with bladder and bowel cancers, allowing them to plan trips during recovery: 'We've had a lot of support from charities such as Crohn's & Colitis UK ... Especially men who have prostate problems [are] appreciative of knowing toilet locations.' In terms of lessons learned, she says 'you need belief in what you're doing. We had a history working in toilet research, so trusting in your expertise and knowing its fallacies is critical ... [We] found the perfect research partnership. Having faith in your team, the person you're working with, is critical. It's your belief in them that helps propel them, helps motivate them. Sometimes the simplest idea is the best idea.' Bichard said that they had a lot of excellent responses from the public and researchers, but they also had problems with people borrowing the idea, without the ability to keep up with the correct data. 'That's one of the biggest challenges: keeping the data up to date and correct ... [We] did get hacked one Christmas, and suddenly 2,000 toilets ended up in the English Channel. We were quite taken with the fact that someone, over Christmas, just thought "I'm going to do this, I'm going in there and doing the toilets." But it was easy to rectify.' She also said that remaining financially viable could be difficult. 'We're entering the innovation space, with projections on possible incomes from a couple of thousand pounds to hundreds of thousands of pounds. But our mission is still to keep the data up to date, raise awareness of toilet provision, and become a useful service.'

+ 001CE/L/01

A grassroots response to a global issue, resulting in an international movement

LITTERATI

+ + Litter is a problem that literally affects all of us: it impacts on the economy, damages the environment, degrades communities, kills wildlife, and is now poisoning our food system.

+ 001CE/L/02

Litter is a challenge faced by everyone: it impacts on the economy, affects the environment, degrades communities, kills wildlife and poisons our food system. Jeff Kirschner conceived the 'Litterati' movement after his daughter spied litter floating in a river, saying, 'Daddy, that doesn't go there.' This initiated a mission to halt what he called 'the world's littering habit'. The concept is simple: take a picture of litter and post it on Instagram, using the hashtag #litterati. Internationally he encouraged people to share pictures of litter, leveraging smartphone 'geotags' (001CE/L/03). The geotag and timestamp features provide location and time data to identify problem areas and enable 'crowdsourced cleaning'. The data creates a bridge to engage companies and encourage organizations to find more sustainable solutions. Litterati has become a shining example of how communities are using technology and data to solve complex problems. Kirschner said, 'It was not hard finding others eager to help rid their communities of mindless litter.' He started to organize tagged #litterati photos from around the globe into a 'digital landfill'. In addition to the 'litter map', the website also presents publicly viewable statistics of litter data. Kirschner added, 'It's not about blaming anyone, it's about sharing information that can create a positive impact

on the planet.' In their statistics, Starbucks' litter is a common subject of the site's trash paparazzi ... which is a powerful message. During interview Kirschner highlighted the lessons learned as being 'resilience and perseverance, following the pain, leveraging existing infrastructures, visualizing data for all ... resulting in action'.

Litterati is a 'community that's crowdsource-cleaning the planet one piece of litter at a time, and through that process, we're collecting quite a bit of data. We're identifying brands, source material, mapping problem areas. The basic premise of Litterati is to create a litter-free world. We think the best way to solve this global pandemic is through building communities, and collecting data, so we can understand the problem.' Kirschner commented that when he was a child, he 'used to go to summer camp, and on visiting day, before they'd let parents come in, our camp director would tell us each to go out and pick up five pieces of litter. When you get a couple of hundred kids each picking up five pieces, suddenly you've got a much cleaner camp.' He thought, 'Why not apply that model to the entire planet?' He started by taking photographs of litter, noticing 'that litter became artistic and approachable'. At the end of a few days, he had 40 or 50 photos on his phone. 'I had picked up each and every piece, and I realized I was keeping a record of my impact on the planet. I started telling people what I was doing, and that one cigarette has now turned into a community in 114 countries, an iOS application, an Android application, and a massive global database of litter (001CE/L/04).'

One anecdotal impact involves San Francisco's desire to understand cigarette litter volumes. Previously the city had instigated a tax to gather this data through analogue processes. Kirschner said that people 'with pencils and clipboards collected information, leading to a 20¢ [tax] on all cigarette sales ... resulting in the city getting sued by the tobacco industry, claiming their data collection wasn't precise, and un-provable'. San Francisco used Litterati's data to not only spend the 20¢ tax, but double it, so that it now generates $4 million in recurring revenue 'for San Francisco to clean itself up'.

Kirschner said that everybody told him to 'follow your passion, and I do believe that's true, but I would add to that – which is, follow the pain. What I mean by that is look for places where people are experiencing pain, where there's a business that is coming up against obstacles, where there are groups who are having trouble communicating. Where's a pain point?' If you can identify that pain point

and provide a solution, 'it's going to make your work that much easier, because you're creating value for someone who needs it. They may not even realize they need it, until you point out the potential solution, which I think is part of what's going on with Litterati, but that would be one thing, follow the pain.' Another valuable lesson is the nature of prototyping: 'It doesn't need to be perfect. It's okay to get started before you have all the answers. In fact, I would suggest that it's critical to get started before you have all the answers, because the reality is you never have all the answers. You must become comfortable in the discomfort. Uncertainty, in a way, becomes your friend.'

Kirschner said that '[the] impact is hard, and sometimes it's not immediately tangible. Sometimes it's not immediately measurable. Sometimes the business models, if you're forming a for-profit organization, or social venture, can be unprepared at first, but stick with it. It's the resilience that is the most critical component to being a social change maker or social entrepreneur.'

+ + If you're going to end up pouring your life into something, you may as well go after something that's really difficult and really challenging, not something that only requires a little bit of effort.

+ 001CE/L/03

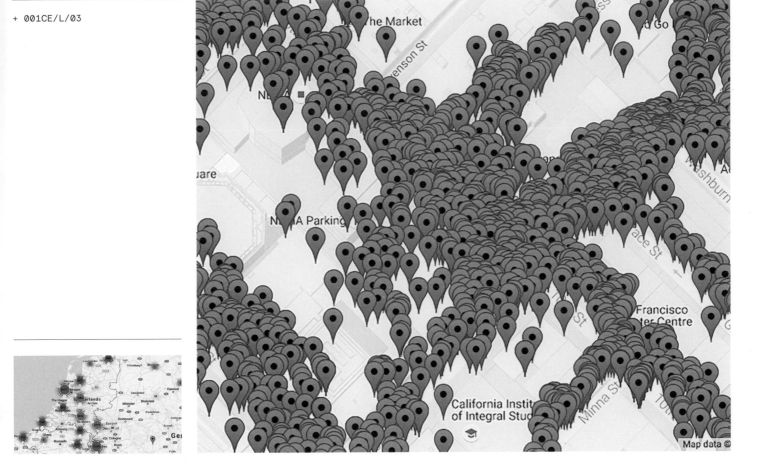

+ 001CE/L/04

+ + We ended up working with San Francisco, providing them with data. They used Litterati's data, generating $4 million a year in annual recurring revenue for the city to clean itself up.

PUBLIC LAB

Encouraging new
models of user agency
through design

OPPOSITE:
+ 001CE/PL/02

+ 001CE/PL/01

Public Lab
Balloon
Mapping
Kit
DIY Aerial Photography

+ + Public Lab are activists, educators, technologists and community organizers interested in new ways to promote action, intervention and awareness through a participatory research model.

+ 001CE/PL/03

British Petroleum's Deepwater Horizon erupted oil into the Gulf of Mexico in 2010, causing catastrophic effects on over 15,000 species, from orcas to endangered crocodiles. It cost lives and shattered the livelihoods of hundreds of thousands of fishermen, oil workers, hotel staff and more, all heavily dependent on the coastline (001CE/PL/05). The company convinced authorities to designate spill areas as a no-fly zone, making it impossible to witness impacts (001CE/PL/03). However, the Grassroots Mapping group collaborated with environmental activists to fly balloons holding cameras over the spill, mapping the devastation. The group used these 'flying cameras' (001CE/PL/02) to collect more than 10,000 aerial photographs showing irreparable damage. Images were stitched together with open-source software, forming up-to-date maps that were more detailed than satellite imagery. Media channels including the *New York Times* and CNN published the findings, with Google Earth also publicly posting maps.

The activists formed the 'Public Laboratory of Open Source Science' (PLOTS or Public Lab, a non-profit). They are a community developing and applying open-source tools for environmental exploration and investigation: consisting of what they describe as 'activists, educators, technologists and community

organizers interested in new ways of promoting action, intervention and awareness through participatory research'. They design with inexpensive equipment and accessible, 'do-it-yourself' techniques (001CE/PL/01). Their community experiments widen participation; relying on people's passion for data, their environment and investigating their locality. PLOTS' manifesto encapsulates the movement's approach that 'products' must be low cost, have data legibility, be easy to use, encourage public participation and creative reuse of consumer tech, and be open source and user modifiable. They involve people and communities without formal training, restructuring the citizen science model, as anyone can contribute. This leverages participants' motivation to explore their surroundings, based on their geographic interests. Jeff Warren, research director for PLOTS, shared his insights.

'The Public Lab was a community before we were an organization. The seven founders of Public Lab met during the BP oil disaster ... [The mapping] kit means lots of things to lots of people. It was a huge disaster; BP and the coastguard heavily controlled it. It was very serious, but also an energizing way [for people to] engage and do things they didn't think we could.' He said that these values are

+ + The fundamental part of Public Lab is helping people see a little beyond their own lives and acknowledge one another's frames. That's cultural work, and it's harder than technological challenges.

+ 001CE/PL/04

embodied in the mapping kit and the process. 'We strongly believe that the objects people create together carry a bit of their essence and ideas. There was something about all the little decisions concerning that kit – how it was taught and learned, how we had events around it, how people thought and spoke about it. That's one reason that it has gone on to live in other places sharing that kind of attitude ... For Public Lab, we think it's really important not to think that technology is just a transformative thing, that's going to change everyone's lives for the better. It's not that technology is the centre. It's the perspective, the people, who are at the centre. How people are able to use technologies tactically and culturally, and make cultural projects that transform relationships and make them more equitable ... [Part] of the balloon mapping story is that people are collecting information more like a photographer than a scientist. They're choosing the photo. The traditional model of data collection is that science is all-seeing, or it systematically collects. Balloon mapping really changes that, because you're going out and capturing shots, exposing something happening (001CE/PL/04). That's more like a reporter than someone processing data, and a sharp contrast with citizen science. People extend the "machine" way of thinking about data collection.'

Warren said that the important lesson he has learned is that their work is cultural. 'People think we're making things, creating technologies, or doing science, whatever that means. We're bringing people together, negotiating collaboration, where all parties gain ... levelling the playing field ... the hardest work is cultural work. Getting people to see that their viewpoint is not the fundamental viewpoint, but to acknowledge the wider story. People's entire lives have often been in a particular cultural frame, and that's difficult to escape.' The fundamental part of Public Lab, he said, is 'helping people see a little beyond that and acknowledge one another's frames. That's cultural work, and it's harder than technological challenges.' Choosing and defining the problem is the first step. 'Framing problems, framing questions, that's one of the most important moments, and it's one that is skipped over in a lot of different workflows or models. Collaborative models really need exploring ... The more we think about it, the more we think of ways to re-engage with collaborative working to define a problem. One difference of Public Lab is the interplay between objects and hands-on processes, on conceptual, political and social ideas. Objects can enable discussions, provide catalysts or open spaces to different kinds of making, which changes these relationships.'

+ 001CE/PL/05

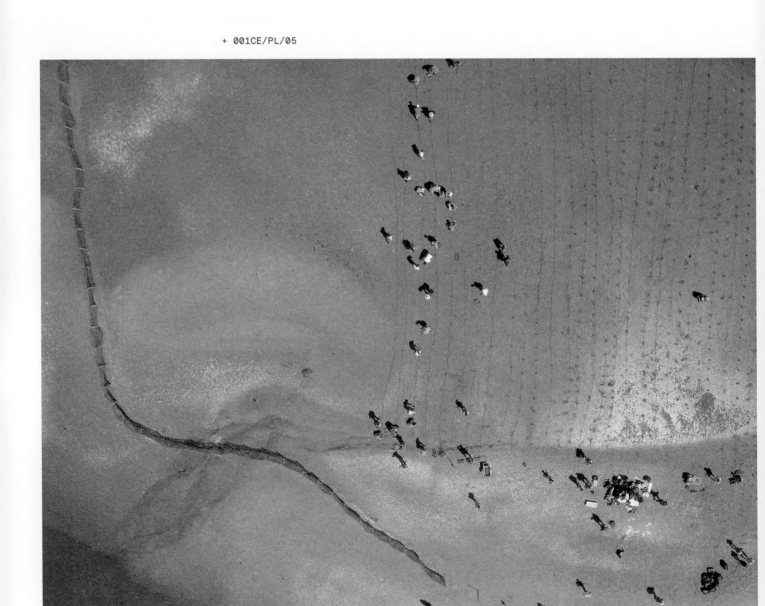

+ 001CE/PL/06

+ 001CE/PF/01

Engaging a community,
designing-out food
waste

PEOPLE'S FRIDGE

+ 001CE/PF/02

The People's Fridge is a public amenity, enabling local residents and businesses to deposit spare food for people in need (001CE/PF/01). It is run by volunteers who want to cut food waste, encourage sharing and tackle nutrition poverty. The offering centres around accessible, cool and secure food storage (001CE/PF/02). Anyone can donate or remove food. The People's Fridge is situated in Brixton's foodie hotspot 'Pop Brixton', whose traders help stock and clean the fridge daily. Similar projects have been launched in Somerset, Derbyshire, Spain, Germany and India. Annually food waste costs the UK about £17 billion, with restaurants alone discarding an estimated 900,000 tonnes of food and households binning on average 24 edible meals a month.

The community fridge concept raises hygiene concerns, but careful design parameters address donation circumstances, minimizing risks. Users sign in to confirm donations and withdrawals. The initiative does not accept raw meat, raw fish or opened milk, and only registered traders can donate prepared or cooked produce. Residents are restricted to leaving packaged food, or unconsumed fresh produce. For example, residents can leave apples but not an open bag of salad, while food traders can donate leftover portions of curry or chopped vegetables. Since its opening, there have been no incidents of people taking advantage of free food. In an interview, co-founder Ben Longman shared his insights.

'[We wanted] the fridge to address two issues: food surplus and food poverty. The fridge is unmanned and free for all to use. We explicitly said we couldn't prevent people taking from the fridge who weren't strictly in need, but we wanted to get people talking about food surplus and poverty. There are organizations that do solid, systematic work in both fields. From the start we knew that a fridge was never going to [rival] those organizations. People have feedback about going to food banks, which do vital and important work. When they go to a food bank, it's not the best day of their life. It's an admission – they can't feed themselves or their family, which is not always in their control.'

When questioned about lessons learned, Longman offered many insights. '[People] talk glibly about prototyping – as in "just do it, fail fast, make mistakes and move on". But the reality is that people don't prototype quickly because they feel it compromises their original vision. We certainly felt that about the fridge, and we faced criticism for putting it in Pop Brixton, a leisure site, aimed at middle-class professionals, not aimed at people in food poverty. But if we had waited for the right site to materialize, we would still be waiting ... [It is] a really great lesson; just prototype the thing. Make your mistakes and get on with it. Another key thing was that we have powered this with volunteers. When we launched the fridge, we had a co-founding team and we knew we just needed more people power.'

The team used the local press and social media channels, 'inviting people to get involved, with a fantastic volunteer response. Often good causes, powered by people, lose puff because the original founders ... move on, they lose interest, something doesn't work, etc. We've got this quite large group of people involved in the fridge, [and they] have real ownership of it ... [The volunteer group are] not just part-time volunteers who dip in and dip out. These are people that really understand the fridge and the social components. Transferring that ownership to people is important, because it's not all about one person. We know other community fridges and initiatives where one or two founders have left, or a paid individual moves on, or the project funding dries up, then the project just dies.'

Longman said that 'engaging people is as important as the end point. You can raise money and pay people, but transferring ownership does amazing things for project viability. We did a lot of press interviews, a lot of engagement; we made the fridge very fun to engage with. And we're still doing that, and we're still communicating a lot about it. I think for people who are involved in projects with a social mission, often that communications aspect is overlooked, because it's hard work just doing the operational aspect. It's hard work just making stuff happen. We found that the fridge is doing some heavy lifting for other food surplus organizations in London, and we willingly do that.' The prime lessons were amenity access and designing out health and safety for community empowerment without fear.

+ 001CE/NGH/01

Co-housing scheme for
older adults

NEW
GROUND
HOUSING

+ + The mission of the Older Women's Co-Housing group stems from a collective desire to take ownership of their age.

+ 001CE/NGH/02

The idea of co-housing arises from Scandinavian ideals and is building momentum in the UK. It enables residents to collaborate in designing and managing their own communities with private areas, while sharing common facilities. It is an ideal form of housing for generations who want to downsize, and/or who live alone (as do 60% of women over 75 years old), but who also want to stay engaged and active. Increasing numbers of older people live alone in unsuitable housing in Britain and remain unsupported and isolated, and this has an impact on health and social care services. Meanwhile, the co-housing process draws on the strengths and skills of older people themselves, sustains their continued autonomy and is based on collaboration and goodwill. The members of OWCH (Older Women's Co-Housing) have been working together for many years, pioneering the idea of a supportive community for women in later life. Shirley Meredeen, 84, who co-founded OWCH, said: 'It's never been done before; we will be running it ourselves and we are extremely proud. We are not going to be a little ghetto of older people, we want to be good neighbours.'

They are increasingly well known as the pioneers of the country's first-ever senior co-housing community (001CE/NGH/02), establishing something that has been a feature of Dutch and Scandinavian life for decades. The architectural scheme has a distinctive character. The entrance opens into shared common areas with communal gardens. The sociable common meeting room, kitchen and dining areas are complemented by amenities including a laundry and drying space with access

for parking and refuse. Tom Reynolds, lead architect, presented their insights. He said their core mission 'was formed from a collective desire to take ownership of their older age'. They came together with a group desire to live together in a mutually supportive community.

'[The] group came with us to site visits and asked us to prepare a planning application ... to work with the Older Women's Co-Housing group, or OWCH for short, in a collaborative design process (001CE/NGH/01). At the beginning, we set about providing this collaborative design process through a series of workshops, starting with design of site layouts, then communal areas, and finally the design of individual flats, materials and appearance of the building. [It was] certainly innovative in the sense that this is the first UK co-housing project for seniors ... [We had] workshops with the group, and then went through the various planning processes. Then we went through the tender process, Quinn were the contractors. The project was procured and, to cut a very long story short, completed in December last year [2016]. All of the OWCH group are now living within the project and setting their own rules, finding out how to live together and alone within their new co-housing community.'

The group was informed by the HAPPI (Housing our Ageing Population: Panel for Innovation) report, which reviewed various case studies for best practice in older people's housing. That document set out best-practice criteria for the future of older people's housing in the UK, setting new standards in terms of

+ 056

+ FUTUREKIND
+ 001 CIVIC EMPOWERMENT

+ NEW GROUND HOUSING

OPPOSITE:
+ 001CE/NGH/04

+ 001CE/NGH/03

daylighting, sociable circulation and flexible spaces that can accommodate a range of care needs, for example if a resident requires a wheelchair or has any other needs in the future, such as private external space. It's part of an ongoing wider discussion around improving older people's housing, aligned with the desire of OWCH to be a purely innovative group and set the bar for co-housing in the UK.

According to the architects, projects such as New Ground are helping to influence policymakers as well as setting the standard for future schemes. Describing the process, Reynolds said that the co-housing group 'were part of the initial designs, and we worked with them to discuss their common spaces within the site layout, how their flats were going to be designed and arranged. Having the end user as part of that process is very important, becoming powerful. Looking at the first diagrams, the group compiled their site

layout – all three groups that we were working with – which was flats arranged around a central garden.' The lessons for the future are about addressing a global health and wellbeing challenge through design, and the strategic engagement of people who will champion the output. The other lessons 'are how we can incorporate innovative housing into part of the wider scope of options in the housing strategy in this country. Perhaps, within that, the planning and procurement procedures might have to develop to accommodate these new types of housing.' The main thread is about challenging traditional models to solve wicked problems of healthcare, exclusion and loneliness, and how these can be tackled through a community.

+ + The Older Women's Co-Housing group came with us to site visits and asked us to prepare a planning application.

002
HEALTH

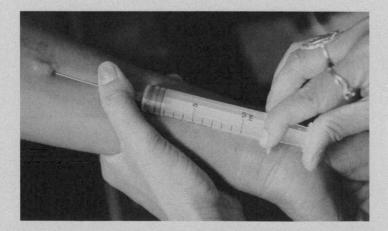

+ 002 HEALTH

COLA
LIFE

Leveraging existing
infrastructures and
systems

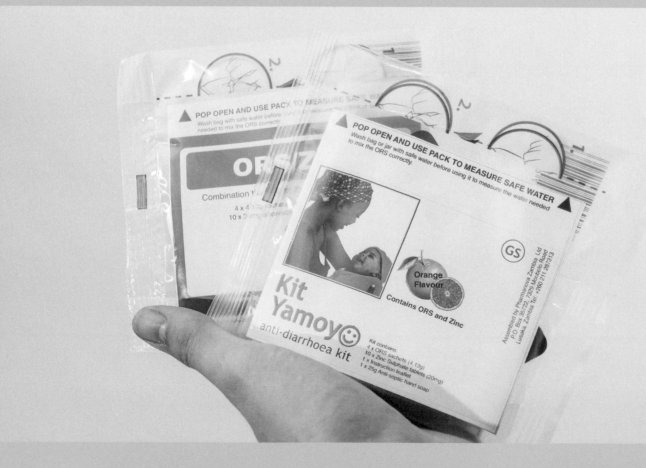

+ + ColaLife's approach for global impact is to influence the strategies of the existing big players in child health, including national governments.

+ 002H/CL/02

You can buy Coca-Cola anywhere in the world, even in remote parts of developing countries ... because it has a phenomenal distribution network. In some of these same places, one in nine children die before their fifth birthday from preventable causes, and most of these die from dehydration caused by diarrhoea. The distribution infrastructure could therefore be used as a medical platform to reach dehydrated children suffering from diarrhoea. With that in mind, Simon Berry, founder and CEO of ColaLife, is working with Coca-Cola to open its distribution channels in developing countries to carry 'social products' such as oral rehydration salts and zinc supplements, to save children's lives. While he was an aid worker in Zambia, Berry asked why Coca-Cola was available even in remote villages, yet simple medicines to treat the second biggest childhood killer, diarrhoea, were not. His wife suggested utilizing unused space in cola crates to carry anti-diarrhoea kits (002H/CL/01).

Simon and Jane set up the ColaLife charity and, from their kitchen table and using social media, won the goodwill of Coca-Cola to scope the concept. Funded by awards, they gave up their jobs, uniting the best minds from big business, academia and non-profits, as well as supply chain experts, health experts, and logistics and design experts. The lorry leaving the bottling plant only goes so far. Beyond the lorry's reach, an army of entrepreneurs take over to carry the product the last few miles to the most remote points on the planet. After a chance meeting at a presentation, packaging expert PI Global took the brief to design a robust pack to carry World Health Organization-recommended diarrhoea treatments – a clever plastic container which, vitally, helps illiterate mothers in rural Africa accurately measure water for the child-sized sachets of oral rehydration salts it provides. The units also contain zinc to help prevent diarrhoea recurring and soap for hand-washing; the pack, dubbed 'AidPod' by the BBC, acts as a cup and a resealable storage vessel (002H/CL/02). Most importantly, 'Kit Yamoyo' was designed with input from African mothers and carers, most of whom live hours from health centres. In Zambia, for a pilot trial, independent rural retailers bought boxfuls, stocking their remote village shops. The uptake happened because it is designed to yield profit, just like Coca-Cola. These retailers, trained by the project team, have, in the last six months, bought over 20,000 Kit Yamoyos to sell at ZMK5 each (just under $1). The most promising retailers are not only serving their community, but also turning a profit of $25–$60 per month ... and in rural Zambia, that feeds a family.

You might not associate 'affordable' and 'well designed' with a kit invented to counter childhood diarrhoea in developing countries. Yet this is what UK charity ColaLife has achieved, through listening to customers and experts. The Kit Yamoyo design benefits have now won over the Zambian Ministry of Health, which placed the first major public sector order for 452,000 kits, to distribute in some of the highest-risk areas of the country. Distribution of the first 30,000 kits is now under way, manufactured locally in Zambia, in an adaptation of the award-winning Kit Yamoyo

OPPOSITE:
+ 002H/CL/03

+ FUTUREKIND
+ 002 HEALTH

+ COLALIFE

+ 063

+ 002H/CL/04

+ 002H/CL/05

+ 002H/CL/06

+ + We aim to generate robust, credible evidence, and innovative and tested designs and approaches, to share with organizations working to reduce child mortality.

design, which has been adapted to conform to the government's branding and requirements. This is an excellent achievement and a major boost for the new product, which contains the established global recommendation for treating diarrhoea with oral rehydration salts (ORS) and zinc. In a customer-friendly design breakthrough, the lightweight flexi-pack offers a measure for the water required to make up each of the four 200ml sachets of ORS packed within it – vital in rural Africa where households rarely have measuring utensils (002H/CL/06). Berry commented: 'Working closely with our packaging partner Amcor Flexibles, we came up with a way to keep the important functionality and attractiveness of our original trial package while ensuring that the kit comes at a cost that won't require subsidy. Then Amcor offered the first 870,000 Flexi-packs as a donation, a saving we've passed on to our local manufacturer and, ultimately, the customer (002H/CL/03).' A trial of the ColaLife

model in 2012/13 increased rates of diarrhoea treatment using ORS and zinc, the WHO/UNICEF standard, from less than 1% to 45% in remote rural areas of Zambia in 12 months. It would have been unethical to stop the supply at the end of the trial, as carers, mostly mothers, had got used to being able to buy ORS and zinc in the form of the anti-diarrhoea kit from their local shop (002H/CL/04).

The value the project offers has increased over time; it is a positive story for corporate buy-in, but it is also a charitable solution that is yielding funds while leveraging a large supply chain. The project has changed from being shipped within the crates to new models of distribution, but the early concept demonstrates that where people cannot give financial aid, they can still offer their capability or existing resource ... something worth remembering.

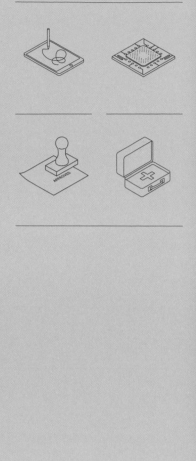

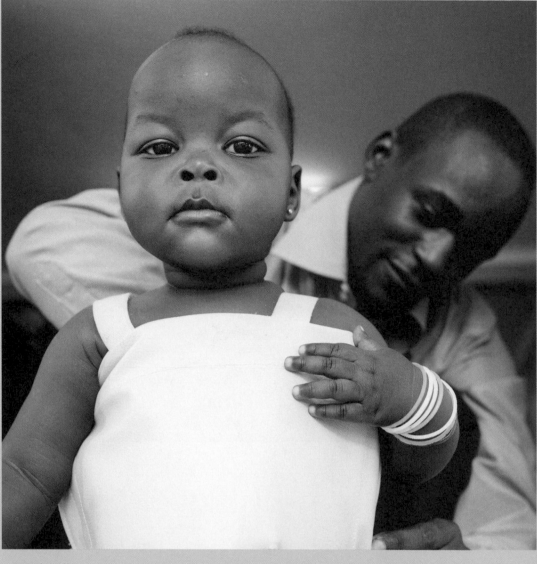

+ 002H/MOJ/01

A tool for early
diagnosis of childhood
pneumonia

MAMAOPE
JACKET

+ 002H/MOJ/02

In Uganda, 16% of children under the age of five are estimated to die each year from pneumonia. Immediate diagnosis could save thousands of lives, especially in poor communities, where health priorities rule out malaria and tuberculosis first. MamaOpe is a biomedical application developed by Ugandan engineers for diagnosis and continuous monitoring of pneumonia patients. Its name comes from 'Hope for the Mother'. The idea came to Olivia Koburongo after her grandmother fell ill, and was moved from hospital to hospital before being properly diagnosed with pneumonia; she later died. Olivia thought of a way in which vital signs of the disease could be tracked in an automated way, and presented the concept to Brian Turyabagye and Besufekad Shifferaw.

Common childhood symptoms of pneumonia include rapid or difficult breathing, cough, fever, chills, headaches, loss of appetite and wheezing. Health professionals are trained to diagnose pneumonia by observing children's breathing rate. This basic method, however, still leaves a diagnosis gap, as different caregivers can end up miscounting the breathing cycles. In advanced settings, a stethoscope can be used (on the lungs) to listen for sounds of infection. However, the engineers discovered through research that pneumonia tends to be at the side of the body, not just in the chest or back, making it hard to locate.

MamaOpe is designed to detect pneumonia at an early stage. It also addresses the challenge of limited personnel in hospitals; the current doctor-to-patient ratio (in Uganda) is 1:24,000. Used with the app, MamaOpe enables audio files to be analysed and compared with existing pneumonia data, determining possible illness severity. Once data is transmitted to cloud storage, other medical professionals, regardless of location, can access the information and assist in diagnosis procedures (002H/MOJ/02). The MamaOpe kit boasts that it can 'diagnose pneumonia three times faster than doctors and reduces misdiagnosis'. It is especially helpful in remote areas or locations where medical resources are scarce.

MamaOpe's core mission is saving the lives of children (002H/MOJ/01). '[We] believe that these [children]', say the designers, 'have a great future in which they can make a huge difference if given a chance to live. Our most important audience is the rural communities where very little is known about pneumonia, and [we want to assist] health practitioners who wish to make faster, informed decisions during the diagnosis process.' The jacket is fully automated, requiring no additional training for the village health teams to operate it. As pneumonia doesn't have a confirmatory test, it is normally diagnosed by checking the signs and symptoms. MamaOpe's kit aims to standardize readings and help health workers avoid misdiagnosis, as well as make custom devices for parents and mothers. They hope to roll out cheap and improved monitoring devices to health centres across Africa, reducing deaths from lung-related diseases. The organization envisages partnerships that make meaningful community impact. They believe that 'social technology can be designed in a way to attract private capital as early as the inception stage, rather than relying solely on philanthropic opportunities'.

The designers also noted that 'there is great need for good partnerships for social technology to make its way into communities. [Rigid] tendencies in regard to the use of technologies should be taken into account, so iteration processes, favouring technology change ... catering for transitions. The strongest impact out of the MamaOpe venture is the fact that we are making an intervention that will radically improve early diagnosis of the largest child-killer disease, i.e. a disease that [accounts for] 19% of all children's deaths globally.' Turyabagye commented: 'Always seek to create enough value for the product; the users will ultimately be ready to add more value to your efforts. And it's best to maintain a thirst for continual growth and learning during every stage of the design and development process.'

The jacket could transform diagnosing, treating and preventing pneumonia in sub-Saharan Africa. Despite international progress tackling measles, HIV and AIDS, and tetanus, funding for pneumonia remains low: for every dollar spent on global health in 2011, UNICEF says, only two cents went to pneumonia. They also say that most of the 900,000 annual deaths of children under five years of age due to pneumonia occur in South Asia and sub-Saharan Africa.

+ 002H/SP/01

Ensuring global
affordability and
designing out fatalities

SAFEPOINT

+ + SafePoint realize that the healthcare worker is the bottleneck, so they try to give them better services and empowering products.

+ 002H/SP/02

Marc Koska OBE is an advocate and global health campaigner who uses interventions to 'design out' global fatalities. During research with the World Health Organization, Koska learned that unsafe injections cause 230,000 HIV infections, 1,000,000 Hepatitis C infections annually, while 21,000,000 Hepatitis B infections result in 1,300,000 deaths a year. His unique innovation transforms existing manufacturing lines to create a modified hypodermic syringe that can only be used once (002H/SP/01). (Syringes, in the developing world especially, are typically reused multiple times, and offer a transmission boost for virulent viruses between patients in hospitals. This was first observed in 1931, with malaria spreading throughout a couple of regiments in the British Army.)

SafePoint's commercial strategy is to target developing world manufacturers, ensuring global affordability, and their technology has established non-reusable syringes as an attainable standard globally. The design was openly licensed and engineered to fit all syringe manufacturing machines, leading to global availability. It has been the driving force behind the 70% cost reduction of safe syringes seen in Unicef's pricing in the last decade. The syringe is approved by WHO and is suitable for curative and immunization markets; in 2008, SafePoint passed their billionth manufactured output. The foundation offers healthcare workers better circumstances to deliver cleaner injections, educating people to ensure medical injection safety.

The unintended consequence of someone giving an unsafe injection was that, three to six months later, they were likely to contract another virus. Koska said: 'People go into hospital with a bad knee, say, and they get a couple of injections while there. They then come out with Hepatitis B, for example, and this becomes a death sentence for their families.' In interview, Koska stated that 'a mother in India won't drink from the same cup, or drink from a cup and then pass it onto her baby, or vice versa. Everyone at the table or in the room, or on the floor will have their own cup because they literally won't do that lip-to-lip possible transmission, because of sanitation reasons.' However, he also said that 'when they go to a doctor, because the doctor is wearing a metaphorical white coat and a stethoscope, suddenly there is this false hope and false trust that surrounds the procedure, and they look away ... I have asked thousands and thousands of schoolchildren in 60 countries: would they share a toothbrush with their neighbour? And they look horrified

OPPOSITE:
+ 002H/SP/03

+ FUTUREKIND
+ 002 HEALTH

+ SAFEPOINT

+ 069

+ + There are many benefits to be had from re-imagining the way we deliver medicines and vaccines around the world.

+ 002H/SP/04

[but] they would go to the doctor and, without a care or a thought, allow that doctor to put anything in their arm.' The mission is to stop disease transmission through minimal product interventions. The main innovation of SafePoint is adopting a licensing model, requiring no upfront costs for a manufacturer; they incur the cost of the small modification to their existing equipment. Subsequently, SafePoint charges the manufacturer a royalty – roughly one fifth to half of a US cent, depending on certain factors – on each product.

When questioned about how designers should respond in these times of social enterprise, Koska said: 'There is no more or less value to a social enterprise compared to an enterprise. If, you know, someone is making syringes and they can make them at the right price and get them distributed – well, then why would they not call that a business? Whereas I am an inventor and I have licensed out. It is exactly the same, just some people try and wrap it up with a different cover.' Koska went on to say that 'we often miss out on the whole holistic chain that accompanies these products, and we lose sight of how many different faults [there] are outside our control. I was prepared to go into them and try and fix them a little bit, which hopefully, I have. It is not always

easy ... Your [designers'] area of excellence is probably something that you can control, but unfortunately, there are lots of other things that you have to control as well to pull it all together.'

The project's impacts include uptake and training in numerous regions and international locations. For example, countless hospitals now only use the K1 syringe. Among others, Koska said that 'SafePoint developed a relationship with Hindustan Medical Devices (HMD) in India, a family-owned manufacturer, which can make quick changes as a supplier to a large area, developing business-to-business relationships.' The business also invested heavily in the training of different medical practitioners; this should not be viewed as a 'Western power' flying in, but rather developing opportunities in collaboration over time.

The most important lessons come from identifying details that can be manipulated in a holistic process (002H/SP/04). The solutions do not require extra training, just product redesign, which involves not only finance but also time, contacts, gaining traction and addressing policy. The design work clarifies the problem, while understanding the deployment economics. The work had a deep research phase, co-created and developed over time for maximum impact.

FAIR CAP

Solving critical issues through social design

+ 002H/FC/01

+ + A vision or an idea can become a magnet, drawing creative and socially conscious people to work together.

+ 002H/FC/02

In many cultures, access to free drinkable water is simply out of reach. Globally, 4 billion people suffer from illnesses and 1.5 million die each year due to limited access to safe drinking water. The social entrepreneur Mauricio Cordova was struck by the Peru cholera epidemic that claimed 10,000 lives in the 1990s. During a visit to the Amazon, he was amazed at how much water was undrinkable. As a result, he wants to eradicate lack of access to clean drinking water through FairCap. A bottle-mounted filter makes water safe to drink; dubbed the 'one-euro water filter' (002H/FC/01), it works with a tested 0.1-micron-pore membrane, removing pathogens like e.coli, cysts, protozoa and sediment. It was collaboratively designed and prototyped using 3D printing (002H/FC/02) and, in the future, could be made locally to promote distributed manufacturing.

In interview, Cordova commented on the lessons learned from the project: '[FairCap wants] to provide pure water for all, in an affordable way, making drinking water accessible even in the furthest places, especially in developing countries. We cater for those who need it most and during emergencies and humanitarian situations like natural disasters, conflicts, refugee migrations, etc.' The FairCap vision empowers people who cannot afford clean water to access it, as a collaborative effort. During his Amazon rainforest trip, Cordova realized that 'even in the most pristine places on Earth, it wasn't safe to drink water from natural streams [or] rainwater, and natural water sources were being contaminated upstream by human activities (sewage, mining,

etc.). That's when the mission started to make water filters for easy transportation [and] usage, and that were affordable – because poor people live in rural areas. Knowing that plastic bottles have unfortunately become ubiquitous, even in remote areas, was the spark to make a small water filter that could fit into a regular plastic bottle, so users [can] obtain water from any source and drink it straight from the bottle without waiting, and without chemicals or electricity.'

When questioned about the future challenges we face, he responded: 'Increased inequality is the major issue in the years to come; that, if not solved, will negatively impact humanity as a whole, creating an elite with access to the best health (i.e. genetic engineering), the most financial resources and most political power, while there will be a large group of people who just live to work and can barely survive. Increased inequality creates opportunities for violent conflict, wars, health risks, pollution, accelerating climate change. How inequality could be reduced from a design point of view could be related to designing systems, services and products to improve education, health, shelter, etc. – but hopefully, by not only thinking of the end user as a consumer, but also as a participant in the design, innovation, funding and making process, especially because of the sheer numbers of people that can be impacted and could become actors in the improvement of their own living conditions.'

FairCap have identified their top lessons and advice in this area: 'Most, if not all, the

+ 002H/FC/03

+ 002H/FC/04

+ + Social design is about imagining solutions that solve critical issues which an under-served part of the population have to overcome.

+ 002H/FC/05

world's top design schools and studios are located in rich, developed countries and cities. [Often] the best design work is done to solve problems that directly impact wealthier individuals. At the same time, there are critical problems affecting billions of people who live in developing countries and poorer areas. Sometimes, it's not a matter of inventing a new technology but identifying needs, considering product accessibility, ease of use, and using readily available technology for scaling, making it affordable even for the poorest people. Design students possess the skills to create new solutions to help billions of people live in better conditions; it is important to understand these needs more, [to] travel and to experience these living conditions and to try to solve those problems. It would be ethical, and it can also create a lot of professional opportunities for new students that are not only financially rewarding but also have a deeper meaning.' When addressing low-income opportunities, Cordova said that 'the key is to design products or services [to] be affordable, not only pitching a low price but a payment system so culturally expensive items can be paid in instalments. Solar energy, mobile phone communications in Africa or private health insurance and education in Latin America follow the latter model. It also means [designing] for the most pressing needs that affect several hundred million people in order to reach economies of scale to decrease the fixed costs of launching a new product. People are willing to invest their few resources if it's about improving their family's lives, their children's health and education.'

The demographics in these sectors ensure a sustainable business model if a new and improved product or service is designed. Cordova said that another way to design financially sustainable and affordable products 'is to design self-assembly, modular and repairable kits, to create business opportunities for small entrepreneurs that become experts and help diffuse a new product or technology. Organizing workshops and training programmes can be another way to sustain a social design project – but hopefully [also] thinking of and designing a system that can be scaled and impacts millions of users; maybe training local experts who, in turn, organize workshops for the local population, making use of online learning.'

+ 002H/O/01

ODE

Stimulating appetite to counter malnutrition among people suffering from dementia

+ 002H/O/02

Dementia poses a challenge to our ageing society and our health services. Currently, 46.8 million people worldwide suffer from dementia, with an estimated care cost of around £400 billion, or 1% of global GDP. Dementia causes cognitive impairment with malnutrition symptoms. Depression, forgetfulness and disconnection from food can lead to weight loss in patients, and associated problems such as dehydration, delirium and muscle wastage. Malnutrition costs the NHS £13 billion annually, with 37% of residents in UK care homes said to be malnourished. Ode is a device designed to address this, which releases food fragrances to stimulate appetite prior to meals being served, developed by Rodd Design and Lizzie Ostrom (of the Olfactory Experience). The concept was part of the Department of Health/Design Council's Living Well with Dementia challenge. The device switches on for a two-hour window around each mealtime, emitting strong fragrances ranging from orange juice to curry, beef casserole to vegetable soup (002H/O/01). This is particularly helpful in advancing cases of dementia where patients lose their appetite and so lose weight, because their senses

diminish and meals become less appealing. Without action, a patient's condition may worsen – but food aroma cues help to prepare people for eating. They stimulate the nervous system, salivary glands and stomach to secrete gastric juices, creating a feeling of hunger.

Ode is programmed to release fragrances by heating bottled scents that are then blown into the immediate atmosphere by a fan. Each 'alarm' is released in waves for at least three hours, so if someone wants to eat at 10am instead of 8am, the scent continues to stimulate their appetite. With help from Ostrom, designers created bespoke fragrances as true to life as science would permit. These 'menus' include comfort foods such as cherry tart and braised beef casserole; fragrances are easily refilled by caregivers, and last three months. A supporting Design Council report stated that '52% of trial participants gained weight after Ode's installation'. Ben Davies, Ode's co-founder, highlighted their lessons and advice, explaining that Ode's core mission concerns 'keeping people happier, healthier and in their own home for longer. Dementia brings a gamut

+ + There were situations where people were concerned that maybe their cats were going to gain weight because they were around food smells all the time. We had lots of anecdotal situations where people were asking for a pint of beer.

OPPOSITE:
+ 002H/O/03

+ FUTUREKIND
+ 002 HEALTH

+ ODE

+ 077

+ + Don't let technology get in the way; focus on meeting the needs of the users. Tech is transient, care isn't. Keep care personal.

+ 002H/O/04

+ 002H/O/05

of problems, social issues and health challenges. We felt that malnutrition is a huge problem among elderly communities; it's compounded if you are diagnosed with dementia. We wanted to see whether we could use fragrance as a simple, passive solution, to try stimulating [appetites, and making] carers' lives a bit easier.'

When asked about lessons he could impart, Davies drew attention to design confidence, collaboration, solution perspective and people. He said: '[The] designers' DNA is seeing the future, making propositions that add beautiful, meaningful, valuable proposals to society. In the UK there is little appetite for that "vision" outside the design community. The bigger challenges we face are due to care being heavily commoditized. We're working with some very open-minded carers and nutritionists, great advocates for the plans, but our customers [the care homes] are not open-minded enough to trial these things. The mantra is to get aligned to an end audience that is open-minded.' His other advice was to 'get that reality check as early as you can (002H/O/05). The reality is that the audience, your customer base, they're just not as receptive. Your story has to be compelling, impact driven and very low cost. If not low cost, then a smart business model so your care community is not your customer. Individuals and parents of those individuals, certainly in [the] dementia space, can become ambassadors and could finance that output.'

'There is a big early-stage opportunity for the dementia space; we called it the "missing stove syndrome". For example, we would go and

visit "Mr and Mrs Smith"; they are holding on to their dignity, trying to live at home. They've got a son or daughter, living half an hour away to pop in, and they've got carers. What you'll see is the kettle and a couple of mugs. You'll open the fridge and you'll see not much at all. You'll see a big slot where the stove was, they're just deemed not safe enough to keep that appliance. We found people who are living at home, which up to a certain point is the best place for them. This was one of the premises for the whole design initiative; you see that people now have to be hungry to order [food].'

They worked with the Royal Hospital Chelsea and the Chelsea Pensioners 'to try and structure impact data using quick prototypes through to placebo situations with more robust prototypes. We were able to influence about 50% to 60% of the cohort [on our test regime], such that we could halt a decline in weight. In some cases we could rekindle an interest in appetite.' Sadly, though, 'everything has to be a metric. Can we provide less human care if we have some automated care? Well, yes, but that moves the problem. Grandma's level of care might be better, but who the hell does Grandma talk to? Last time I looked, Ode doesn't speak (002H/O/04).'

FOLIA
WATER

Providing access to safe
drinking water for all

+ 002H/FW/02

+ 002H/FW/03

+ 002H/FW/04

Access to safe drinking water is a basic human right. However, currently 3.4 million people die annually from water-related diseases such as cholera and E. coli, and 99% of those deaths occur in developing countries. The organization WATERisLIFE is aiming to combat water-related diseases through The Drinkable Book™ (002H/FW/01). Imagine a book with pages you tear out and use to turn raw sewage into drinking water. Each page is implanted with silver or copper nanoparticles that kill bacteria when water passes through, and the pages are printed with messages in local dialects, for example: 'The water in your village may contain deadly diseases. Each page of this book is a paper water filter that will make it safe to drink.' The filtration system has been shown to eliminate 99% of bacteria in water during field trials at 25 contaminated water sources in South Africa, Ghana, Kenya, Haiti and Bangladesh (002H/FW/02). To clean water, users tear a page out of the book, slide it into the accompanying filter box and then pour water into the box, passing it through the purifying paper. Each filter can purify 100 litres of liquid, meaning each page could last for weeks and each book could last for roughly a year.

The project started during Dr Theresa Dankovich's PhD. Afterwards, she developed an appropriate design for users in developing countries. The Drinkable Book concept is a partnership between WATERisLIFE and the ad agency DDB NY. It has evolved to become the more practical Safe Water Book, which includes simple graphical instructions and a versatile funnel filter holder. Their global vision is to reach the 1.8 billion people who consume microbiologically contaminated drinking water as well as the 2 billion people who pay the 'poverty penalty': overpaying in time, energy or money to obtain safe drinking water. Lack of clean water is catastrophic for public health: diarrhoeal illnesses kill more than 500,000 children a year. Folia Filters™ kill waterborne pathogens at a price that is affordable even to those who make $1–10 per day. The filter paper has been scaled to industrial paper machinery, and is being tested in sales trials in Bangladesh and Mexico.

Dankovich described the way in which social technology 'incorporates novel ideas into products or services that consider the needs and desires of [the] target market segment. In our case, we used human-centred design principles to evaluate various filter designs and created our minimal viable product through extensive target customer feedback.' The important element is the 'minimal viable product' option that can scale but also strategically take the organization in an appropriate direction, testing a market. They described their impact as an early-stage company: 'We have stirred the imagination of many people outside of the typical communities for humanitarian efforts. We have had an outpouring of people coming to us to try to help grow our impact around the world.' Their biggest lesson has been to 'listen first, then design solutions'. This empathy is an overarching design fundamental that applies universally. They believe that businesses should strive to create technologies and designs that are affordable to the entire bottom segment of consumers from the start: 'The capacity of NGOs and charities typically hits the lowest economic level of the income pyramid (the humanitarian market; around one billion who earn less than $2 per day). However, there are many more people who earn between $2 and $10 per day that can also be potential target customers and are more likely to be able to buy products than [those in the] humanitarian sector serviced by the NGOs.' The project reviewed a challenge to produce the lowest viable product option through accessible means; a simple narrative for users, investors and media traction.

MAKE HEALTH

Offering people the opportunity to design, make and produce design interventions that meet their own personal needs

OPPOSITE:
+ 002H/MH/02

+ 002H/MH/01

+ + We were intrigued by the intersection of basic healthcare and the maker world, so we initiated MakeHealth.

+ 002H/MH/03

+ 002H/MH/04

+ 002H/MH/05

MakeHealth is a project in which citizens, healthcare professionals, designers and makers co-design and co-develop open, innovative and personalized healthcare solutions (002H/MH/01). The partners at MakeHealth explore how stakeholders in healthcare can be creators of solutions that support the care process and that contribute significantly to patient empowerment (002H/MH/02).

As this futuristic landscape becomes reality, the regulation system should evolve likewise – but it hasn't yet. However, this lack of evolution is not (yet) stopping innovative makers designing (002H/MH/04). This is because, in the context of open design and DIY, official approval is not required. As long as you bypass the market and make or re-make something for your own use, anything is possible. There are potential litigation issues with this type of work; however, the team are pushing ahead in their field with active public engagement, looking for low-barrier entry points. Initially the MakeHealth partners are interested in the design and development of open healthcare solutions, in relation to legislation and standards, to provide more governance and agency.

Program developer Paulien Melis (Waag) shared her insights: '[With] cutbacks in insurance and more active participation of citizens (002H/MH/03), we think people need help in different ways, as [often in this medical field] either there is no solution, it's very expensive or the solution doesn't work. We were intrigued, as if you combine basic problems of healthcare and the maker approach it provides user agency, so we initiated MakeHealth. Users are good at articulating their needs, but often they don't know the process to resolve a new solution. That's where the fabricators and designers support this collaborative process of creating solutions. If citizens with a healthcare challenge or healthcare professionals develop solutions, it could have international impact. We are trying to seed local solutions and openly document concepts for wider engagement.' Melis describes their mission to facilitate 'people having the confidence of "self-innovation" through a reliable ecosystem to self-manage and improve their quality of life'. One example of this 'self-innovation' is a 3D finger splint: 'It is a tool for hand therapists

or physiotherapists. They measure the finger on specific elements, and with a parametric model the splint is personalized. They send it to an e-certified printing company to create personalized finger splints for patients.'

When questioned about repeatable insights, Melis responded that 'often value is not talked about enough. People consider monetary value; they don't always think about existential wellbeing, or job creation ... or the output of people being more invigorated or confident. Secondly, it's really different to collaborate on health-related solutions, for example working with a severely disabled child really pushes your empathy, it pushes your whole view of how you interact with people, your working practice. It's taking little steps ... [one of the] main issues here is the open sharing and documenting of solutions. There is not a good platform at this moment where people can source solutions. Either they're showcased – you can't reproduce them – or you need to scavenge. It's a scavenger hunt to find suitable healthcare solutions because you end up with furniture and Halloween decorations. A platform for health solutions is really timely. Because healthcare is one of the most regulated areas you can be working in, we must consider ethical aspects: what happens when you create a solution and there is an injury? We need to debate as citizens, as individuals on how we cope with liability. What are the risks that you are personally willing to take? That's a debate that needs discussion.'

'If we want to innovate or progress, we need to change the way we approach healthcare innovation. This is also aligned with the whole self-management and participatory way of thinking. The government is really pushing healthcare to citizens themselves. This is the debate that needs to be had, because it's ethical and you are the person responsible for your health and wellbeing. It is crucial that if you are involved in the solution, you have ownership over the solution.'

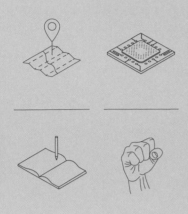

+ 002H/VD/01

Creating a link to
expertise through
infrastructure

VIRTUAL DOCTORS

+ 002H/VD/02

Virtual Doctors (VD) is improving access to specialist healthcare and advice for communities in rural Zambia that are desperately in need (002H/VD/01). However, the stimulus for the improvements began in tragic circumstances. Founder Huw Jones, working as a safari guide, was driving through a remote area and happened upon a cycling couple ... the man riding and the woman on the handlebars. She was pregnant and bleeding heavily, in intense pain after travelling for hours to reach a hospital almost 60 miles away. Mr Jones drove them, but the woman was already weak and tragically died in the back of the vehicle before reaching medical help.

This user-centred system is a telemedicine intervention combining software and internet-connected smartphones, linking local clinical officers with volunteer doctors (002H/VD/02 and 002H/VD/03). This results in quicker patient diagnosis, and often people can be treated in their own communities, reducing the need for journeys to distant hospitals. The initiative is now live in numerous Zambian locations. The process engages specially trained clinical officers to screen patients prior to them seeing doctors, using a mobile app to submit patient files electronically. The software enables clinical officers to build confidential patient files to send to medical experts in Zambia, the UK, the US, India, Pakistan, China, Nigeria, New Zealand or Malaysia. Patient files include their details, medical history, prescription(s) and answers to specific questions from clinical officers. This system is using mobile connectivity to change how healthcare is delivered. In an interview, Lina Woehrling shared her team's insights.

+ 002H/VD/03

'[The project] took years to mature because technology had to catch up for this to become tangible. During that time, Huw had been talking to doctors and to clinical officers in Zambia, to work out practicalities. They developed a pilot, using satellite to connect a volunteer doctor in the UK with an isolated clinical officer in the rural clinic in Zambia. You probably know that satellite is very expensive and can be unstable, apparently due to birds sitting on dishes. Rather than attempting video links, we created a patient case file, with information uploaded to the cloud. [It was] picked up by a volunteer doctor, who could respond to it with

their advice and [enable] the clinical officer ... to respond with further questions.' Their core mission, she said, 'is to use technology to connect remote communities with volunteers elsewhere, helping their patients and promoting education as well as mentoring.' Their long-term vision is to hand over the service, 'to locations where it is most needed, managed by the local ministry of health and local doctors clustered in the cities, helping the clinical officers, who are in the remote areas'. The idea is that 'they do not need Westerners' help'. One of their biggest impacts has been the educational legacy: 'Jonathan, one of our clinical officers, has provided the most patient cases. Since the passing of his father, he has been wanting to become a clinical officer, possibly become a doctor eventually, which is why he is a great user of our service; he loves all the continued education he takes away from this. This is really what we want from our project. We want our beneficiaries to take ownership of it.'

Their repeatable insight is that 'non-profit will always attract more help ... and pro bono [support] ... because this was not about capital venture, it was not about making money, it was literally about helping others, an attraction we've been able to drum up – you just need to see all these volunteer doctors, who have flocked to help us provide the service, it is just amazing.' They are currently having trouble, 'because [the] efficient scalable model, (an elegant solution) is having issues ... with the devices. Problems with bandwidth, and our clinical officers on the ground are struggling to make the devices work. We are currently trying to get some funding to pay for in-country support to the project manager who is there, who can go and find them, deploy and maintain the devices. And for us to hammer home the fact that with our job base established, you cannot build anything else. In a world where tech is increasingly important and where it opens so many doors, but it is also very fragile and it is really easy to fall down ... and you need to build it up again, and the smallest technical issue, the smallest Novell software update, can knock everything down. You have to be really cautious with that, it is a bit of a double-edged sword. Tech issues often cannot be predicted, and you cannot predict when they are going to happen.'

+ 002H/DC/01

Providing knowledge and choices for future generations in a culturally acceptable format

DIVA CENTRES

+ + The genius part of doing nails was having conversations about sex without making eye contact.

+ 002H/DC/02

+ 002H/DC/03

In Zambia, access to contraceptives and sexual health information is difficult for teenage girls. Diva Centres provide adolescent girls with knowledge, informing their decision-making and enabling them to control their future (002H/DC/01). In a country where, on average, one-third of women give birth by age 18, access to reproductive health services is paramount in ensuring girls have the opportunity to finish school, start their career or become mothers on their own terms. Diva Centres give young women a safe, comfortable environment to learn about birth control, confidentially, from trained peers. At Diva Centres, girls do their nails while having informal conversations about sex. They hang out with friends, and when they are ready receive counselling and access to short- and long-term birth control in a safe and judgment-free environment from trained professionals (002H/DC/03). The Diva Centres were designed by IDEO.org with Marie Stopes International in Zambia (MSZ). With colourful furniture, magazines and a range of nail polishes to choose from, the centres feel more like nail salons than clinics.

'[We know that] unintended pregnancy is a problem in Zambia; it's the second-leading cause of death for young women. When you're struggling, and then have a baby at age 16, it makes the likelihood of changing your situation harder ... [The core mission] is to connect contraception and their ability to access contraception, to [help them] take control over their lives, and to [give them] greater agency and an improved ability to get themselves out of poverty.' The work was initiated with the Hewlett

Foundation 'working on the issue of young people amid rising youth populations, especially in sub-Saharan Africa'. IDEO.org partners with organizations that are experts in their fields and that have the capacity and ability to implement at scale – in this case Marie Stopes International. '[We work] together to build an offer that's going to resonate with young women, and in this case young women in Zambia. What has been amazing is that we've increased the number of young women they're serving by 16 times.'

The project was grounded in user-centred design, which the designers said means '[we] go out and say, "If we are going to look at how to answer this issue of increasing contraception for young women, let's understand young women." We have to understand their lives – their parents, their culture, what's motivating their behaviour and driving their decisions.' The Diva offer is threefold. First: 'It's a brand/message connecting with young women, presenting contraception in a memorable way [and] connecting with how they perceive themselves. The second part connects teens to the sexual and reproductive health services they might need. You go there with your friends; it's a teen-owned space. The genius part of "doing nails" was having conversations about sex without making eye contact.' Finally, the third part 'was to realize [that] no one knows how to talk about sex to teen girls in Zambia better than themselves. That material already spreads verbally, but often through misinformation, so equipping teens with facts gives them agency over themselves.'

+ 088

+ FUTUREKIND
+ 002 HEALTH

+ DIVA CENTRES

OPPOSITE:
+ 002H/DC/05

+ 002H/DC/04

IDEO.org was asked to share project lessons, and they responded with a mix of cultural understanding, collaboration and removing preciousness. '[We] often get questions dealing with cultural differences between staff, located in San Francisco and then working in Zambia. The truth is, it's always a challenge, and will remain [so] until we resource designers from Zambia (002H/DC/04) ... When you show up as a person, with respect and willingness to collaborate, you get to see people as people, and it is possible to truly relate to folks.' There are so many reasons why culturally we're the same: 'We all care about our futures, we all love our kids; we all enjoy a good laugh. They are as important as the things [that are] making our worlds different.'

'[You] should not be precious and not be afraid to try things, build, experiment and learn. We came to the nail salon [idea] through a research technique. Our team was trying to say, "How do we get girls to talk to us about sex and about the realities of what their lives are like around this question that can be pretty taboo? Let's try to create environments where they feel comfortable talking to us," and so they actually set up pop-up nail salons and advertised: "Come get a free manicure." The research technique was so effective it inspired

the actual solution ... [Things are] going to fail, but some stuff is going to work, that's what you hold on to and build around. It's about not being precious; it's about building things and trying lots of ideas, bringing everybody along for that journey. The stakeholders were learning, building and were creators alongside us. Marie Stopes International continue to run and implement Divas ... they own what it is.'

+ + The way we approach design is very much to go out and say, 'If we are going to look at how to answer this issue of increasing contraception for young women, let's understand young women.'

+

003ENVI
MENT
+
SUS
TAIN

+ 003ES/F/01

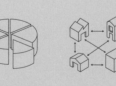

FARM BOT

Removing the
knowledge barriers
to home farming

+ + # If you can build IKEA furniture, then you can build and use a FarmBot.

+ 003ES/F/02

+ 003ES/F/03

The Trussell Trust, responsible for stopping hunger in the United Kingdom, stated that in 2016 it distributed 492,641 meals through food banks to low-income families. Food poverty is not something that is happening in distant countries. Over the past few years, food-bank usage has increased across the country. Dieticians often comment that the UK population was healthiest during the Second World War, due to rationing and the prevalence of allotments, vegetables and regulatory diets. But over the last ten years, allotment uptake and the number of people growing their own food have rapidly increased, according to the National Allotment Association. And it is only a matter of time before food production becomes more automated as modern life changes.

Robots are already deployed on our farms; for example, milking machines save labour and increase yield. Arable farmers use GPS to map crops, monitoring yield, weed incidence and other data, and robotics and farming are becoming closer bedfellows in other ways. Meanwhile, modern farming is often criticized for its depleting effects on the land, chemical use and potential impact on wildlife. For people who would like some control over the provenance of their food, but lack the skills and time to manage this, FarmBot is a personal robot farmer. It is the first open-source CNC farming machine intent on creating an open and accessible technology that can help everyone to grow food (003ES/F/03). It runs on open-source hardware such as the Arduino Mega 2560, and involves community contributions on a wiki and forum. There you

can find documentation, schematics, assembly guides, troubleshooting tips and more. A system costs $3,100 (£2,400) – quite a high initial investment for families. However, the company plans lower-cost devices in the future.

The robot is built from corrosion-resistant aluminium, stainless steel and 3D-printed plastic to operate in harsh outdoor conditions. FarmBot is like a giant 3D printer, except that instead of extruding plastic, it uses seeds and water to grow crops (003ES/F/01). Similar to 3D printers and CNC mills, FarmBot hardware employs linear guides in the X, Y and Z directions, which allows for tooling such as seed injectors, watering nozzles, sensors and weed-removal equipment to be precisely positioned. It can run off mains electricity from a wall outlet, or be powered with a small 100W solar system. If it encounters problems or power loss, the owner is notified. An onboard camera and software monitor the garden, detecting weeds as they emerge, and burying them under the soil.

Users log in to a web-based app, dragging and dropping their preferred plants on a visual grid to plan a garden with 33 crops to choose from. The software is pre-loaded with details such as plant spacing, adjusting automatically without effort from the human farmer. According to founder Aronson, the outdoor unit can be constructed to fit the owner's individual requirements. It can scale from a garden as small as 1 square metre to a farm as large as 20 square metres. In terms of cost, the maker estimates that a FarmBot can run on anything from $1,500 to $4,000, depending

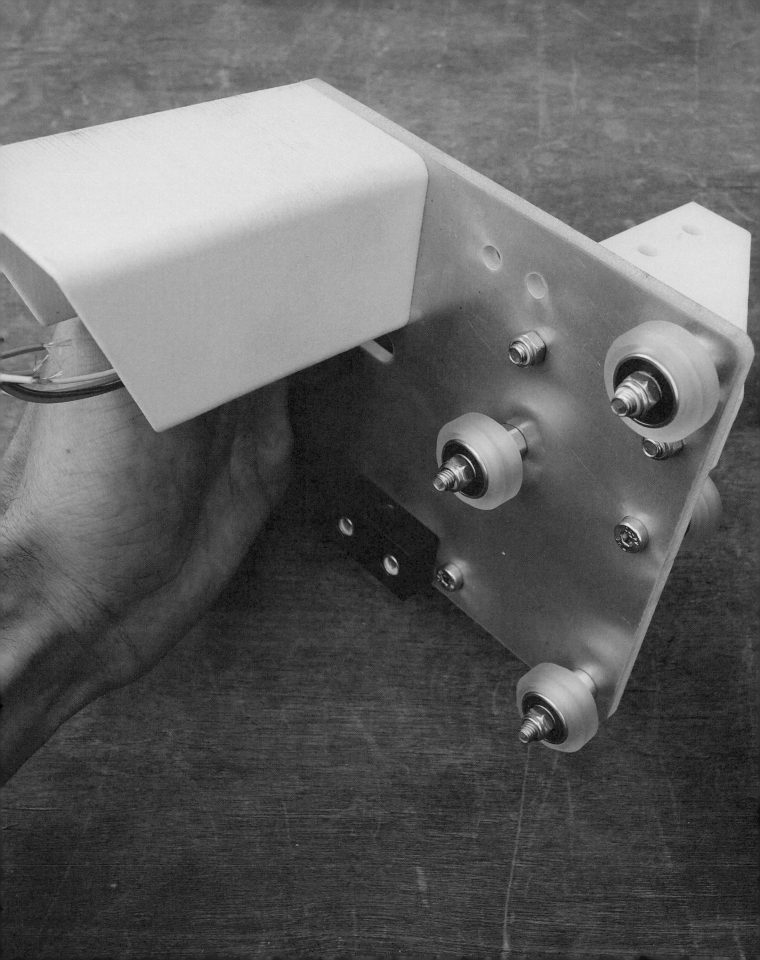

OPPOSITE:
+ 003ES/F/04

+ FUTUREKIND
+ 003 ENVIRONMENT
    + SUSTAINABILITY

+ FARMBOT

+ 095

+ 003ES/F/05

on installation size. FarmBot combines basic operations in custom parameters for seeding and watering, and enables users to build complete regimens for a plant throughout its lifetime (003ES/F/05). Features include storing and manipulating data maps, accessing an open plant data repository, and real-time logging. An integrated support system automatically adjusts water, fertilizer and pesticide regimens, as well as handling seed spacing and timing based on soil and weather conditions, sensor data, location and the time of year.

The project has its challenges: the high cost of the unit against people's annual salary; the pleasure that people take in growing food and their proximity to technology, which creates discomfort among traditionalists; the idea that people should be actively engaged in their food production; and new developments will always encounter pushback (003ES/F/04). Furthermore, there is the physical wear of the units in different climates to consider, as many 3D-printable materials, at the time of

writing, will not withstand the extreme weather present in some locations. Finally, for today's generation, it is plausible that people will contribute to local food production, possibly taking responsibility for their borough, as food gardens are increasingly populating our schools and verges through guerrilla gardening.

This trend should be viewed through the lens of development and empowerment. Yes, there are issues: the group is using an open platform to create a movement that can be scaled. They do not state the direct audience and must not only be seen through the eyes of a domestic user, but also with the potential for scale, or application, to complement local urban retailers over time. Yes, there will be issues with insects and the possibility of creating weak species, but this is a step-change with potential. This project is a gateway to a new form of urban farming, in locations that are unfit for other activities or difficult to reach, which will encourage more people to grow their own food.

+ + We are focused on anyone who wants to grow food in a way that requires fewer barriers to entry, less transportation, and hopefully less water and time.

+ 003ES/FP/01

Ethical, traceable
manufacturing that
helps us maintain the
goods we own

FAIRPHONE

+ + FairPhone's mission is to make the smartphone industry's supply chains more transparent.

+ 003ES/FP/02

+ 003ES/FP/03

OVERLEAF:
+ 003ES/FP/04

Disposal of mobile phone handsets results in millions of units annually becoming landfill. As a consequence, many countries are establishing e-waste recycling programmes and sorting broken electronics. However, goods are also routinely exported to developing countries, which lack formal recycling facilities, and are subsequently burned or landfilled, releasing harmful environmental toxins. FairPhone is an ethical campaign to increase material circularity awareness, and awareness of conflict mineral use in everyday electronic products (003ES/FP/03). 'Conflict minerals' fuel and sustain armed violence in the eastern Democratic Republic of Congo (Congo), linking them to the deadliest global conflict since the Second World War. The four conflict minerals (gold, along with the 'three Ts' – tin, tantalum and tungsten) are the most lucrative sources of income that go to arm guerrillas. Laws enacted from 2010 created requirements for all companies trading in the United States with products containing any of the four conflict minerals to be regulated. Compliance costs were grossly overestimated by industry lobbyists; an independent environmental consulting firm estimated that the total cost of compliance was approximately $140 million (2014).

FairPhone's values of long-lasting design, good working conditions, fair materials and circularity are transforming the electronic industries playbook (003ES/FP/01). The Democratic Republic of Congo produces at least 50% of the world's cobalt; this is used in lithium-ion batteries, which power smartphones and electric cars. Consumer electronics

manufacturing is demanding, involving labour-intensive production processes. Living wages, health and safety, and legal representation all need addressing. To effect positive change, relationships must be mutually beneficial and transparent, with manufacturers investing in employee wellbeing, in which FairPhone is taking a lead. Smartphones contain over 30 different minerals, and all minerals and metals enter supply chains through the mining sector – a challenging industry for environmental and social responsibility. Many 'mining-related' practices need addressing, including pollution, dangerous working conditions and child labour.

FairPhone are striving to advance our 'product relationship' over time, reviewing product economies, and holistically evaluating supply chains: from conflict-free tin sourced from South Kivu, Democratic Republic of Congo, which provides the solder for conductivity, to Fairtrade gold sourced from Peru. They believe supply chains should be traceable, ethically based and benefit surrounding communities. With over 100,000 products sold, and 50 employees, they are a growing organization. FairPhone also develop their manufacturing employees through a welfare fund, promoting training and skills development. Users are becoming more interested in products they purchase and use, forcing manufacturers to respond. It is plausible that manufacturers and retailers will have to make repairable products in the future. FairPhone therefore offer a step-change in the form of the repair of personal goods, with an online parts repository to replace broken components operating within warranties,

+ + We're campaigners at heart, and that's why we're passionate about leading with our values.

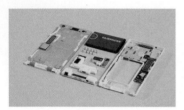

+ 003ES/FP/05

and legal ramifications protecting both parties. FairPhone also partnered with iFixit (producer of custom 'hacking' tools for corporate technology) to create repair guides and offer professional repair services (003ES/FP/05).

The second agenda is material and supply chain transparency. FairPhone openly publish all their componentry sourcing, materials and mine origins on a publicly accessible source map. Within the repository, users can locate factories supplying any component, linking to gold mines with conditional information and locations of tin mines used for solder. It is visionary to openly publish suppliers' data, encouraging community scrutiny. In this way FairPhone are bringing more fairness to software, in line with their overall design objectives. Their software focuses on openness, transparency and ownership, and they are intent on achieving greater product longevity.

They launched code.fairphone.com, an open-source development website from which developers can download source code and drivers, and access FairPhone build information. While creating developers' kits is not new for hardware manufacturers, FairPhone are encouraging technical experts to become involved in their community. They commented: 'In future you will also find instructions on how to contribute ready-to-use builds, maybe including your contributions [in the product].' This outlook is empowering users to develop the objects they own and use. FairPhone was one of the first to embrace 3D printing, giving users the ability to 3D-print

their own cases, and partnering with providers to print on demand. The interesting concept, however, is not in aesthetics, but in distributed manufacture, with sites located around the globe or in your corner shop. It eliminates the need for long-distance shipping and the production of excess stock, while giving buyers opportunities to interact with local communities to gain a deeper understanding of product or material provenance.

FairPhone had many vital lessons to impart. Primarily, they said, producing everything under Creative Commons licence opens up community opportunities to build on work, placing trust in developers. They hoped that in time users would take more responsibility for what they buy, use and dispose of; these behavioural changes will require major change, though, and the common 'mobile phone' is a great start point. It is promising to see over 112,000 happy customers with 150,000 community members supporting their global goals. FairPhone are tackling e-waste, a complex issue with global ramifications. They have partnered with 'Closing the Loop', providing solutions for e-waste in countries without formal electronics recycling. They are also developing e-waste awareness campaigns in Ghana and have collected 75,000 discarded phones to ship for safe recycling. FairPhone's aim is to grow the world's supply and demand of recycled materials, by increasing recycling and encouraging suppliers to buy recycled materials (003ES/FP/06).

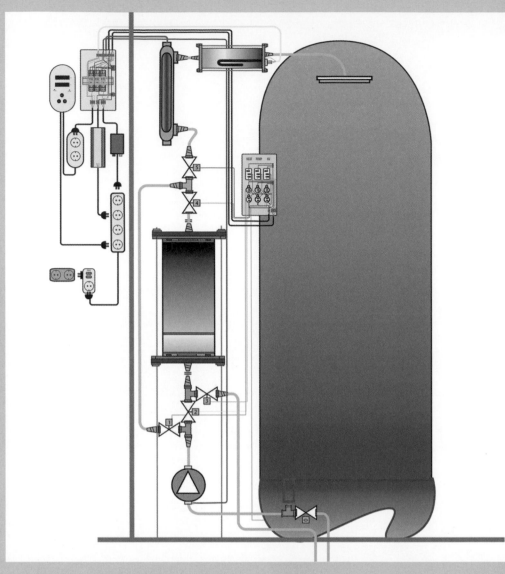

+ 003ES/SL/01

Careful redesign of
an everyday item to
address water usage

SHOWER
LOOP

+ 003ES/SL/02

Finland-based designer Jason Selvarajan felt guilty about taking long showers and decided to address the issue of water wastage. As a result, during POC21, a sustainable innovation camp, the Showerloop project was upgraded from a hobby to a mission. Instead of water flowing away, the Showerloop retains the water, sending it through numerous filters to clean it before pumping it back through the shower head (003ES/SL/01). The water circulates in a loop until the person using the shower finishes. The steps involve a screen and microfibre to filter out hair and larger objects; sand filters out particles; activated carbon removes smells and chemicals from the water and, finally, ultraviolet light kills bacteria. Because the water is already heated, it takes less energy to keep it hot as people use it. Selvarajan stated: 'The recycled water meets or even exceeds US and EU drinking-water standards.' The start-up is selling DIY kits, and the design is open source, accessible to those with the skills to make it

(003ES/SL/02). The designer commented: 'It allows for [a] better lifetime of the product because users can fix it themselves, making it with local materials and services.' The design currently uses around one-tenth of the energy of an existing shower. The device can be installed inside or outside a shower or bath. The main components are a pump, sand and activated carbon filters, and a UV lamp. The system is made from an amalgamation of parts that can be found in hardware shops around the globe. Showerloop is designed to retrofit on to your existing shower system, so there's no need to remodel your home.

The project is built from common materials and tools found in a fab lab. The filters can last as long as two years with daily use, depending on the quality of the soiled water. The sand filter can be washed; the activated carbon (AC) can be regenerated (but only at high temperatures of more than 500°C) or composted; and the

+ + Showerloop is a water filtration and purification system that recycles shower water in real time, allowing you to shower with hot water for a long time but only use 10 litres of water per shower. Showerloop can save you 33,000 litres of water and 1MWh of energy per person per year.

+ + The fab lab has empowered me by giving me the tools to take what's in my head and make it real.

+ 003ES/SL/03

+ 003ES/SL/04

+ 003ES/SL/05

+ 003ES/SL/06

+ + 90% reduction in water usage
and 70–90% energy reduction for
a 10-minute shower with a flow
rate of 10L/min. Savings depend
on user behaviour and can vary.

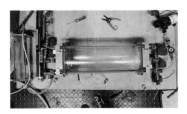

+ 003ES/SL/07

UV lamp should last for thousands of hours but can be recycled and replaced like any other compact fluorescent lamp (CFL). The design of the product is modular (003ES/SL/05), making it easy to repair, replace and find materials (003ES/SL/07). The constraints come from the filter dimensions and power output of the UV lamp, but Showerloop can save around 33,000 litres of water and 1MWh of energy per person each year. The world is changing, and we need to evolve our approach and habits. Showerloop is one element of a sustainable lifestyle that can also scale, for example in the leisure and hospitality industry, to have a large effect. The next step for the company is to understand the human issue and ensure that communication empowers customers and makers.

The following interview with the founder, Selvarajan, highlights lessons to be learned and how we need to embrace these changing times. Selvarajan explained that the project was born from a homework assignment 'after calculating the heat-recovery opportunity of a shower that recycles hot water (without filters at the time) and uses a heat exchanger to warm water for a cleansing final rinse. We pretended that the product existed with some basic mock-ups (003ES/SL/06) made in SketchUp, and our classmates seemed to buy the concept ... [The core mission] was to just enjoy a guilt-free hot shower, but then I realized the potential impact it could have for the billions of people without access to clean water and sanitation, [taking into account] the growth of cities and the global population and the need for it all to happen sustainably and economically. I figure we either need something like fusion power or a way to reduce energy consumption without decreasing the quality of life and the enjoyment of things that makes us build civilizations.'

Their biggest lessons have included ways to leverage existing systems, resulting in sustainable behaviour change. Selvarajan advised: 'Be curious, ask lots of questions and find people and places to work. You don't have to have a lot of money to do it. There are lots of tools and materials just sitting around waiting to be used; you have to find and liberate them.' He highlights the need to do things as sustainably (both socially and ecologically) as possible. 'Maybe sometimes that means not making things as well. For me, it's all about open source and efficiency. Waste not, think in cycles, clean up after yourself and help others. I keep thinking about how broke I am but how much fun I have meeting people at the fab lab, learning about their projects and how things work. I think if we all had access to the right tools and made things that mattered we could stop the planet from melting and have a good time doing it.'

SMART HYDRO POWER

Working with nature to provide power

+ 003ES/SHP/01

+ 003ES/SHP/02

Smart Hydro Power started as a group of kinetic turbine developers with experience in remote/off-grid locations supporting simple, competitive and complete design solutions (003ES/SHP/01). They believe in sustainable development, empowering people to define and shape their own lives. The Hydro turbines are designed to enable complete renewable-energy solutions in rivers and channels. Their patented technology is standardized and expandable, as the products are positioned as an alternative to decentralized electrification. The Smart Hydro Power turbine was developed to produce maximum electrical energy through the kinetic energy of water currents.

The turbines do not require dams or water height difference to work, keeping watercourses in their natural state, and not requiring infrastructural investment. The amount of kinetic energy (velocity) varies from river to river; the greater the water flow, the more energy is generated. The river turbine system is modular (003ES/SHP/02), enabling integration with multiple sources, and the project has expanded into other offers that include kinetic energy, agricultural production and photovoltaics. The sources complement each other using sophisticated control systems to ensure stable electricity generation. In interview, CEO Dr Karl Reinhard Kolmsee shared the team's knowledge.

'The project started when I was working in Peru, selling biogas plants in the Amazon. I came across farmers asking for "a device enabling them to use river energy". I thought it must exist, because it's obvious – [to] not dam water, but utilize its flow. [But] even though the technology is not new, the product did not exist … [Our core mission] is to develop a kinetic hydro power plant, sold to people who develop projects. We design and commercialize kinetic hydro power plants, packaging these plants with photovoltaic and distribution systems. The devices are used to bring complete solutions of rural electrification. We are a local utility bringing technologies to the most remote places, mainly in Latin America.' Smart Hydro's strongest impacts, he said, 'have been in Peru, as it's a project where you have difficulties getting the devices to remote areas, as our turbine weighs 350kg. Remote does not mean

"a dust road", it means you have to ship it with small boats and it's often many shipments. We went to a village (near Iquitos in Peru) and they had never seen or experienced electricity. We installed a system with the community. After two weeks of [providing electrical power access] to the community house, residents started collecting oranges. They mixed foraged orange juice with crushed ice, [and] were selling juice to villagers passing by on the river, gaining independence; a step [towards the] social and economic integration of the country.'

Kolmsee said that '[it] takes longer than you would expect at the very beginning … You will run out of money. You will have a device that doesn't work. [But] as long as you work together with beneficiaries, with users, you can ensure it works and is really giving something of value to people. If you don't ask people, you may have a wonderful, technical device but you can't be sure they will use it or buy it. [The] process of asking people is not easy. The first thing I ask new interns is how would they calculate whether a river is fast enough and deep enough [for our technology]; they usually respond "go there and measure it". Going there means you spend €2,500 on transportation. Then "I communicate with local residents, asking them how fast it is." You have to ask people whether they can still swim [against it]. Whether they can go through, and then you get from their real-life experience an answer that helps you to develop your technology. Developing technology means first listening to people and trying always to translate between the language and the experience people really have, and the language and the experience you have … [You] may have read that GE and Siemens are suffering with their electricity and power business. Both companies have a fantastic track record in terms of using the best engineers. But both companies have lost the track towards modern generation. They produce fantastic photovoltaic distribution panels and wind turbines, but they don't understand that people: a) need smaller units and b) [find them] too expensive. Our work environments in India and Latin America mean finance is limited. It's being honest [about] whether we are able to bring something at accessible cost to a community that really works. If we cannot, then we shouldn't promise it.'

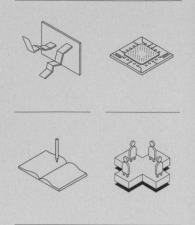

+ 003ES/GL/01

Designing with local
resources, questioning
product architecture

GRAVITY
LIGHT

+ + The reality is, if you are going to steer a venture to have genuine impact, you need to navigate very carefully.

+ 003ES/GL/02

+ 003ES/GL/03

GravityLight uses kinetic energy to produce light (003ES/GL/01). It is an affordable, reliable and safe alternative to kerosene lamps, used by 1.1 billion people globally (003ES/GL/02). Kerosene consumes 15% of the income of the very poor. A single kerosene lamp burning daily for four hours emits 100kg of carbon dioxide annually. According to the World Health Organization, 3.8 million deaths a year are attributed to household air pollution, caused by people burning kerosene and biomass fuels for their energy needs.

GravityLight is powered by lifting a weight – a bag filled with 12kg of rocks or sand. As the weight descends, it turns a gear chain that powers a dynamo, creating light instantly. After 25 minutes, when the bag reaches the ground, it can be lifted again, as required. GravityLight has been designed through iterative prototyping, testing and user trials. The company want to create a modular system that can power other devices, from radios to mobile phones, tailored to the user's needs. The original specification paid for itself in weeks, with a 3-second lift giving 25 minutes of light (003ES/GL/04). To build a sustainable, scalable business while ensuring products are affordable and accessible to low-income households, the price of the light varies by country. In the UK it sells for £64.99, while in Kenya it was sold for 2,500Ksh (c. $25). Once installed, it costs nothing to run, meaning GravityLight could pay for itself within 50 days of switching from using kerosene lamps.

Jim Reeves, GravityLight's co-founder, imparted his insights during an interview. 'The idea for GravityLight was conceived in 2009 as we looked for a way to create a lower-cost solar lantern. The battery and photovoltaic panel made up the majority of the cost of a solar lantern but, unsurprisingly, the cheaper these were, the worse the product performed and the shorter their lifespan. So we considered alternative sources of power that were not reliant on the sun. This led us to experimenting with dumbbells and bicycle wheels to test how much power could be produced from biomechanical energy. What could be more freely available, worldwide and any time of day, than human power? We had managed to create a system that could provide instant light, independently of the weather and which was not dependant on the lifespan of a battery. The increasing efficiency of LEDs meant that the less than 0.1 watts of power produced by this system would be able to produce light several times brighter than a kerosene lamp.'

'Our commercial model also requires ongoing testing and iterating to build a sustainable and scalable approach. Our aim is for GravityLight, and future products, to contribute to local livelihoods, rather than risk undermining them through giveaways. In such price-sensitive markets with some very hard-to-reach rural off-grid customers, this creates a whole new set of challenges. From a product-development point of view, there is an extremely tight balance to be struck between cost, performance and longevity. And, as GravityLight represents an investment for our customers living on little more than $3 a day, it needs to be attractive and elegant too.'

+ 003ES/GL/04

+ 003ES/GL/05

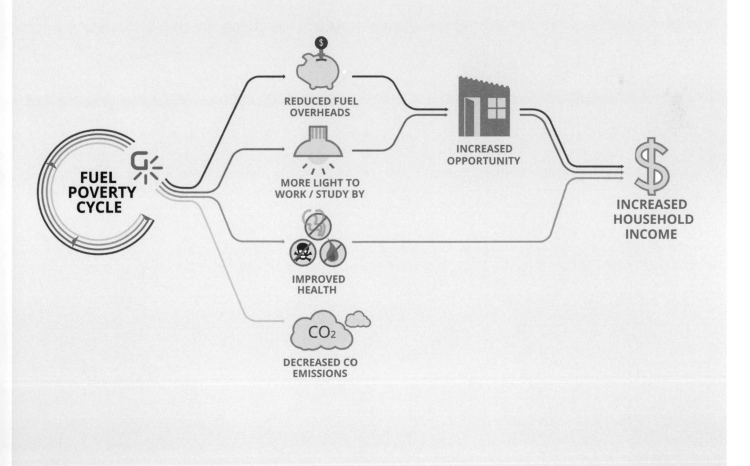

OPPOSITE:
+ 003ES/GL/06

+ FUTUREKIND
+ 003 ENVIRONMENT
    + SUSTAINABILITY

+ GRAVITYLIGHT

+ 113

+ 003ES/GL/07

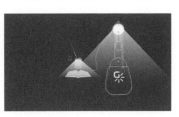

+ 003ES/GL/08

+ 003ES/GL/09

+ + We wanted to get this refined to a product proposition that could be distributed on a bicycle; raising a bag of rocks as your energy storage worked for numerous reasons.

'In GravityLight's manufacture, we wanted to test whether local assembly was feasible and the impact of this on creating livelihoods as well as on the total product cost. And we've also tried a range of sales and marketing approaches, with different pricing and payment models. In Kenya, 93% of the population have a registered mobile money account with MPESA, which has transformed the ability of the "unbanked" to send, receive and save money. These tools, combined with community savings groups – "chamas" and "saccos" - and increasing access to credit have transformed the ability of low-income households to invest in products with longer-term benefits and savings, rather than being limited to the cheapest and, often, worst quality.'

'It will take until 2080 for there to be universal electricity access in sub-Saharan Africa. Off-grid energy solutions are a central part of the mix to provide people with access to clean, safe and affordable energy. And while "value for money" will always be an important calculation to any consumer, as we look forward to future product development and improvements, the increasing availability of finance will be central to further increasing and accelerating access to electricity. As users save money over time through solutions like GravityLight, they can then invest in their family's wellbeing, education or businesses, as well as progressing up the next tier of the "energy access ladder".'

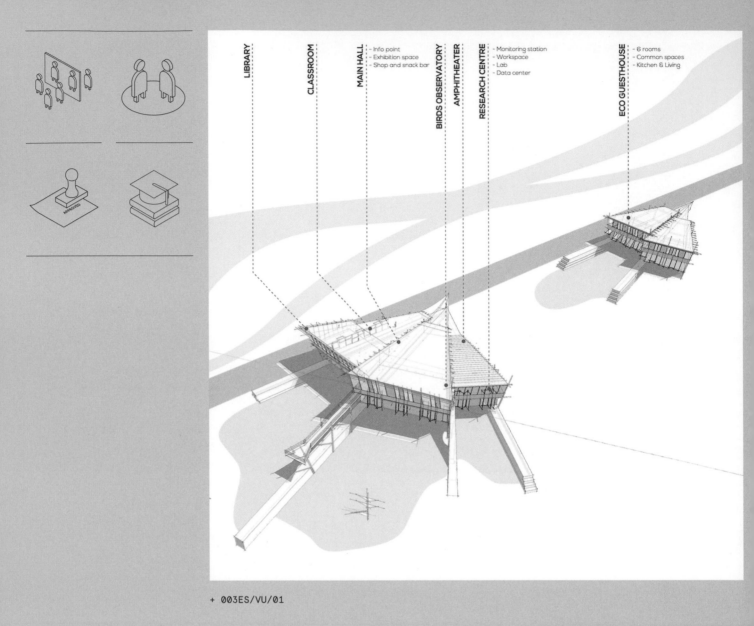

LIBRARY

CLASSROOM

MAIN HALL
- Info point
- Exhibition space
- Shop and snack bar

BIRDS OBSERVATORY

AMPHITHEATER

RESEARCH CENTRE
- Monitoring station
- Workspace
- Lab
- Data center

ECO GUESTHOUSE
- 6 rooms
- Common spaces
- Kitchen & Living

+ 003ES/VU/01

A platform for nurturing
community-informed
biodiversity

VERTICAL UNIVERSITY

+ 003ES/VU/02

+ 003ES/VU/03

+ 003ES/VU/04

The Vertical University creates 'living classrooms' in a 7,600-metre continuous vertical forest corridor, stretching from Nepal's largest aquatic bird sanctuary to Mount Kanchenjunga (8,585m) (003ES/VU/01 and 003ES/VU/02). It is a vessel to teach and conserve, with 6,600 flowering plant species, 800 bird species and 180 mammals found in eastern Nepal. In Nepal, there is exceptional biological, climatic and cultural diversity, from the tropical plains to the Himalayas. The 'professors' of the Vertical University may not have PhDs, but as indigenous farmers they possess deep knowledge of local fauna and flora. They seek to deepen place-based skills in sustainable technology, craft and medicinal plants, and conserve and activate local knowledge to nurture sustainable livelihoods. Their mission is to promote biodiversity, conservation and environmental learning. The professors work with non-profits, in classrooms called 'Learning Grounds', each governed by a diverse local board and monitored by the Social Welfare Council (SWC) of the Nepalese government.

In interview Priyanka Bista explained the vision. '[Our] approach to conservation is to tackle root causes of biodiversity and habitat loss, such as the lack of rural livelihoods [and] inadequate research, planning and inventory work. Our most important audience are the local stakeholders (003ES/VU/03) including students, youth, farmers and teachers ... [We train them] in how to map, monitor and inventory biodiversity by interviewing local farmers, using reference materials. [In] Nepal, conventional education paradigms where students sit in a stationary classroom, divorced from the surroundings, make little sense ... [It] is becoming difficult to raise funds for charities and NGOs around the world. Therefore we need to think about alternative approaches to sustaining projects in the developing world. Financial mechanisms are critical to ensure longer-term sustainability of projects ... [Nearly] 40% of the youth population – more than 5 million young people – are unemployed in Nepal. Many are migrating overseas to take low-paying, low-skilled jobs, often in dangerous working conditions in the Middle East and Southeast Asia. As low-level migrant workers, many end up working in harsh construction sites with little to no workers' rights.'

'We have focused on hiring and building [the] capacity of local youth in all project aspects. Ganga Limbu, a 21-year-old girl who is also landless, joined our BELT fellows programme with very little knowledge of computer programs. Today, as the Mapping and Research Fellow, she has learned Adobe Premiere, ArcGIS, AutoCAD and SketchUp. She learned methodologies to design surveys [and] collect data on GIS Pro and Kobo Collect. She learned to analyse data in Excel and is learning scientific dissemination ... [and] to document videos using DSLR cameras and editing software. [Professionals] and students working in this field need to go into communities with humility and respect towards local stakeholders. We need to begin with a collaborative spirit, finding partners who can engage in all project areas from the beginning. The responsibility of a design professional interested in social design doesn't end at the drawing board. We have to invest in the process.'

Participatory design is still not engaging communities enough by hosting one-off charrettes or workshops, but is beginning to work in collaboration to develop those charrettes or plans. Bista said that '[there's] a gap between designers and builders, or designers and communities. Our approach might be different because we bring the community in from the beginning ... [The] difference from other groups is that we involve people at every step, through the Youth Fellows programme; we're training youth in the work and spreading skills ... [The] developing world ... is urbanizing at a rapid pace, resulting in complex socio-economic and political problems. To operate within this field, we have to comprehend the complexity and interrelatedness of challenges.' He said that design needs to move beyond architecture into engaging complex socio-economic systems. For example, interconnected problems require systems thinking, bridging gaps between 'us' and 'them', bringing stakeholders to the table from the beginning, thinking about handover and exit strategy from the very beginning, and engaging in environmental problems that move beyond traditional environmental solutions (003ES/VU/04).

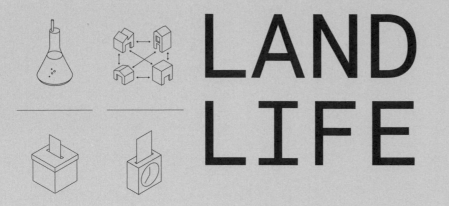

LAND
LIFE

Designing tools
for sustained tree
replanting

+ 003ES/LL/01

+ 003ES/LL/02

The Land Life organization enables trees to grow in arid conditions, using their 'Cocoon' (003ES/LL/01). The Cocoon is cheaper than traditional planting techniques, and it dissolves into an organic substrate after planting. It removes the need for follow-up irrigation while supporting seedlings during their infancy. The units provide water and shelter, promoting a healthy and deep root structure that taps into sub-surface water supplies. To date, trees planted with the Cocoon (in more than 20 countries) have survival rates of 80–95%. The process produces independent, strong trees without reliance on external irrigation, capable of surviving harsh conditions – and the paper pulp construction biodegrades in a year (003ES/LL/02). The Cocoon can be used in projects of various sizes, for different species and soil compositions. Planting helps restore ecosystems damaged by overgrazing, tree cutting, droughts, floods or industrial/mining activities. Restored ecosystems improve rainwater, provide shade, increase the soil's organic matter content and enhance soil life. These interventions also enable vegetation to grow around planted trees, often increasing the land's value. In interview, directors Arnout Asjes and Charlotte Jongejan shared their insights.

'[Land Life use a] technology over 2,000 years old for growing trees in dry areas. Historic cultures buried clay pots underground to slowly deliver moisture, irrigating saplings by the roots of a tree. That process provided water access protection, preparing the saplings for independent life in nature. With irrigation techniques and high-intensity farming increasing, it has become a different story, [forcing reliance] on irrigation in areas where there is no water available ... [We] use the same technologies, but make it biodegradable; that is how we developed the "Cocoon" ... [We have planted in more than 25 countries, witnessing numerous] 'different uses, different interventions that we can do. We're still

+ + We use a technology over 2,000 years old for growing trees in dry areas. Historic cultures buried clay pots underground that slowly delivered moisture, irrigating saplings by the roots and protecting water access, preparing the trees for independent life.

+ 003ES/LL/03

+ 003ES/LL/04

+ + Trees planted with the Cocoon
(in more than 20 countries) have
survival rates of 80–95%.

+ 003ES/LL/05

looking at hundreds of hectares of land that are dry, which is our biggest competitor – there's nothing to do. It's too dry. The past couple of years, with climate change, it really has become too dry (003ES/LL/03).'

'[Our] ambition is to forest, reforest, replant hundreds of millions of hectares of degraded lands. We're seeing climate change … it's getting drier; people are migrating to cities. I'm not saying our product is a silver bullet, but we can install pioneering vegetation in dry lands … it replants trees.' Land Life's core mission is to restore the world's 2 billion hectares of degraded land (003ES/LL/05): 'Of those 2 billion hectares, about 1 billion is arid; the super-remote, drought-stricken, degraded soil that no one wants to touch is our objective … [For] scale, 2 billion hectares is the size of the US and China combined, and every year we lose another 24 billion tonnes of fertile soil. The problem isn't going away; it's increasing. We work with NGOs, governments and private clients; at the end of the day we're restoring degraded land.'

The strongest impact has been in 'the "Green Refugee Camp" in Cameroon, where we are planting in a refugee camp (003ES/LL/04). [From an] ecological, organizational, social, political [point of view], every aspect of our work is extreme there. Working in African countries is always different from working in Europe or the US. The complexities of working in a refugee camp, [with its own social] priorities, conflicts and personal histories, we can't even begin to fathom. Socially there is a need for reforestation in areas witnessing hot, dusty,

eroded [conditions], scarcity of food and lack of shade. Providing a long-term project not only through planting trees, but working with UNHCR and camp organizations establishing tree nurseries that continually produce seedlings for years, training their refugee community to become proficient in seedling propagation. Trees are, on the one hand, harmless … who doesn't love a tree? But it also indicates permanency, making it a symbolic thing … you're putting down roots. Finally seeing the "Cocoons" go in the ground has been satisfying. There are 40,000 trees going in the ground.'

The lessons learned by Land Life include finding that 'flexibility is an important attribute. We advise exceptional planning, but [to] be ready to throw it out the window and think on your feet. The team is critical. We are a company of doers and thinkers. We have people from McKinsey background, with strategic thinking, combined with on-the-ground thinking. Being able to combine skill sets often helps us to come up with a solution that one person alone wouldn't have, but also two of the same types of people wouldn't have. We do have some really different characteristics in the office, ranging from someone who's a real data specialist, to arid agriculture workers from Israel, to communications backgrounds.'

+ 003ES/WT/01

Design with unskilled
makers in mind

30 DOLLAR WIND TURBINE

+ FUTUREKIND   + 30 DOLLAR WIND TURBINE   + 121
+ 003 ENVIRONMENT
  + SUSTAINABILITY

+ 003ES/WT/02

+ 003ES/WT/03

There are plenty of options to enable off-grid living, for example wind turbines, solar panels, generators and so on, but all these require funds, which presents a social access challenge. These challenges fuel POC21, an innovation camp for ventures developing sustainable solutions. The group hand-picks interventions in energy, housing, food, water and mobility, providing makers with space, time, tools and resources, supported by world-class mentors. Made from bike parts and discarded aluminium, the 30 Dollar Wind Turbine (003ES/WT/01) is exemplary of POC21's work. Daniel Connell designed it to have a small footprint and a big output. If you have a spare bike wheel and 30 bucks, then this can reduce your ecological footprint (003ES/WT/02). The project delivers a few hundred Watts – enough to pump water. Connell stated that anyone who 'can cut paper and hold a drill' could manage it. Construction involves cutting aluminium into shapes, then bending and riveting the vanes to a bike wheel. Connell previously designed an open-source solar energy collector that cost around $100. Built together with the turbine, it develops energy independence. This project can be used to pump water or air, run a cooling system, or charge a battery through a generator. Connell focuses on upcycled and reclaimed materials, making his outputs affordable and accessible (003ES/WT/03).

This is not a mass-manufacture project, but is designed for 'community reclaim and assembly'. In interview Connell identified the challenges. '[The prototype] was pretty easy to assemble, but came up against the standard wall ... access to land to plug it in and fully use and test it. I spent time developing the workshop model and just giving the things away and working within existing projects ... [The core mission statement is] radical accessibility, basically whatever people need they have to have access to. Here in Guatemala I came in with the model of doing workshops, showed up at the project and asked "What's needed here?" I didn't go in with preconceived notions or requirements ... [I'm] not expecting 99% of people to make their own stuff, but if one person picks it up as a job and makes 100 of them and sells them, then everyone's having one. That person is incentivized, establishing a micro cottage industry. It also means that

people making the "product" are geographically located to maintain and optimize it. The idea of "What happens when the thing breaks?" isn't really addressed, because you just better chuck it out ... rip the parts out of it, use it for something else. That's because it was mass-produced in a factory in China ... The locals didn't make it, so how are they going to fix it? If they did make it then they can fix it, improve on it and roll it out to a wider region. The key necessity for that is that there be no overheads to cover, for all intents and purposes. That materials are super-cheap and locally abundant. You don't need to invest in a whole bunch of tools and machinery or skills; you just follow the recipe. You have the thing then you understand the thing better because you have now made it and so you can distribute it.'

Connell explained that he had to 'simulate the entire process and build that into designs. Once you get to these places you realize you didn't know anything about them. All the cultural needs, the realities on the ground and the social needs. I am process designer. When I talk to professional engineers I piss them off, because they're "You can't do that", [and] I respond, "What you said makes complete sense from a structural and machining perspective, but we're not designing for ideals." [I find that] engineers need to be deprogrammed before they can engage in this process because they've learned how to do things properly, without considering things that happen in the real world. You have to design stuff which can be badly made and still perform in a safe, efficient and productive way. [It is] not just a matter of getting a prototype to function, let alone to market; you have to build the accessibility into the entire thing from the start. When designing you have to think of the materials [and] tools and consider the ergonomics of the build process – where people will be putting their hands – and whether people can work alone or require assistance.'

'I never went to university, so I don't have a formal education. I'm not good at making and I haven't addressed it because ... I'm designing for other people like me who don't know what they're doing. I keep seeing labs pop up as the only higher-education group who are engaging, but they "over tech", so there's not a lot of just buy-parts-and-tinfoil-like building going on.'

ECO WAVE POWER

+ 003ES/EWP/01

+ 003ES/EWP/02

The Eco Wave Power (EWP) energy converter is an inexpensive technology for generating electricity through the power of waves. EWP buoys are intended to be located on unused piers, breakwaters and other coastal structures. They are designed to 'blend in' with their surroundings, while also helping to reduce shoreline erosion. The technical equipment is located on land, preventing it from being dislodged, improving reliability and providing easy access for maintenance (003ES/EWP/01). The equipment's location does not interfere with the sea bed, and has no impact on the marine environment. The system gathers energy from waves, converting wave motion into fluid pressure, which is then fed through pipes to power plants for conversion into electricity.

The system is being developed to produce electricity in a cost-efficient manner. This is achieved by using mostly off-the-shelf, well-priced materials and reducing maintenance costs. The device consists of two different buoys that rise and fall with the waves, and which are connected to supporting structures via arms and a hydraulic cylinder. The system is 'intelligent', monitoring the ocean environment to recognize prevailing storms, and autonomously deciding whether to lift or submerge the equipment above or below the water. The 'intelligence' also adjusts the buoys' angle, optimizing and maximizing energy generation (003ES/EWP/02). Co-founder Inna Braverman offered valuable insights.

'[The company] was co-founded by myself and David Leb. David was attracted to wave energy because one of his investments was a surf camp in Panama. Being there, and seeing the power of the waves, he developed a passion for this field. Wave energy is the future, because the density of water is 800 times greater than [the] density of air, so you can produce more electricity with much smaller devices ... [There is an] ongoing race between wave-energy developers. There are about 200 companies out there, trying to develop a commercially viable and reliable wave-energy solution with limited success, which made us want to be the first company to deploy a wave-energy power station successfully. That was the beginning of Eco Wave Power ... [The] first mission is to make a better planet, make a cleaner planet for the future generation.

According to the World Health Organization, one in eight people in the world are dying a premature death. Obviously, all of us want to take care of the next generation, and we want to make sure that we learn how to harness the natural resources that nature has given us, in order to make our lives and our children's lives better ... [The] second mission is proving that renewable energy is not only good but it can also be profitable ... [Wave energy] didn't commercialize for many years. People always thought it was too expensive, and non-reliable; a big objective is to prove its profitability.'

'We opened our first commercial-scale [installation] at the power station in Gibraltar. It is the first time in history that Gibraltar [has] received any renewable energy from waves. It couldn't install wind turbines in its territory because of bird migration, so really the best solution for them was to harness the power of waves. It will have a great influence on the people there: instead of burning diesel, which is their main source of electricity supply, they can receive some of their energy from waves. We also hope it will help to change the world's perception of wave energy ... Once we had opened the Gibraltar station, we proved that the system can be protected against storms and that it will not break; also, to prove its commercialization potential, we built it for a very low price in comparison to offshore wave technologies.'

Braverman stresses the importance of having a really good understanding and picture of the field: 'A lot of the competitors in our field that are developing renewable-energy technologies are engineers. Sometimes, I think, engineers have difficulties connecting what they learned in school, as well as thinking outside of the box ... I think if they took everything they learned in engineering [class] but also learned how to think outside the box, outside of the closed lines, thinking in a more creative way, then a greater success could be achieved ... [We] think that everything that we are taught cannot be challenged, but checking, researching and examining the things that are learned [is vital].' In short, Braverman believes that new processes and methodologies for unlocking creativity are key to greater social outputs.

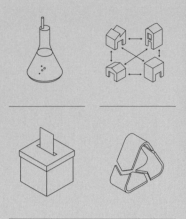

+ 003ES/PT/01

Training drones to
identify waste plastic
in the ocean

THE
PLASTIC
TIDE

+ 003ES/PT/02

One of the major barriers to solving the plastics pollution issue is that we simply don't know where the plastic is. Of the 10 million tonnes (and rising) that enters our oceans globally every year, less than 1% is visible. The other 99% is missing, with only sparse or inconsistent anecdotal evidence about its distribution in our oceans and along our coasts. This hampers any initiatives to legislate against littering or effectively distribute clean up efforts. The Plastic Tide has therefore adapted drone technology to survey beaches using machine-learning algorithms, to remotely and autonomously identify plastic waste. The founders have collated 20,000 aerial images and are 'training' the algorithm in plastic waste identification, with the intention of scaling up the open source system globally (003ES/PT/02). Qualified drone pilots will be invited to contribute images for instant analysis, in a process that will soon be capable of detecting up to 90% of beach plastics (003ES/PT/01).

This large-scale citizen science project is exploring the relationship between and impact of plastics on communities and individuals. Co-founder Ellie Mackay shares the charity's insights. 'When we first talked about doing something large-scale to clean beaches, we realised that emerging drone technology could massively speed up the process. Our research then led us to discover machine learning as a new way of identifying objects automatically.' But they faced a challenge: how to train the algorithm specifically to detect plastics? They trialled citizen science portal Zooniverse with positive results, leading to the launch of a massive data-gathering exercise all around the UK. Ellie Mackay explains 'The technology allows us to detect, monitor and even predict marine plastic distribution, building a global hotspot map that will inform policy-makers, academics, local clean up groups and activists all around the world. Our mission is to create a "digital eye" for humanity, to provide a critical and

+ + The 'plastic tide' is growing by 8 million metric tonnes a year ... without action, it is estimated that this will rise to 80 million metric tonnes a year by 2025.

+ 003ES/PT/03

+ 003ES/PT/04

+ + Bringing citizens along can't be underestimated – the importance of getting people on board, as well as technology and science.

+ 003ES/PT/05

scientifically robust tool for cleaning the oceans and preserving paradise for generations."

So far they have surveyed beaches in several countries, including a 4,200 mile trip around the UK coastline. (003ES/PT/05). 'We collected thousands of survey images and now have over 5 million classifications from our citizen science community of 10,000 volunteers. The idea scales well, sustaining impact through innovative ways of environmental monitoring and coordination of clean-ups.'

When questioned about their transferable insights, they highlighted the importance of team collaboration and deep specialists (003ES/PT/04). Co-founder Pete Kohler told us '[It] was a build-up of expert engagement, and that's the fundamental nature of The Plastic Tide: bringing experts from different fields together to solve a problem, and then watching the magic happen. Within the project there are deep specialists in respective areas. If you're a student who's a deep specialist in one area, I'd advise you to identify what you're good at, whether that be programming, communication or design skills, and find an idea that inspires you, making you want to find out more, to explore and test yourself. Go to events; meet other people inspired by the same things. Our commonality is that we all love technology, science and the environment, so when we combine all three it allows us to build a powerful project.' 'Given the challenges we face as a planet, the collaborative and holistic solutions offer the most potential. These challenges are fundamentally not unique to a specific

profession. We think the future lies in building complete solutions, particularly as we're becoming a more environmentally conscious society, and there will be more challenges arising in the coming decades. The Plastic Tide combines marine science, machine learning and deep learning mixed with drone technology, mixed with environmental challenges, in a unique and innovative way. As well as bringing the public along, that can't be underestimated – the importance of getting people on board, as well as technology and science.'

FARM
HACK

Responding to food–creation challenges

+ 003ES/FH/01

+ 003ES/FH/02

+ 003ES/FH/03

+ 003ES/FH/04

Food acts as 'social glue' – joining communities, economies, healthcare and families. But its production is being pushed to breaking point, and it will require active participation to ensure that 'big agriculture' and government are not in sole control of it. A community of farmers, designers, developers, engineers, architects, roboticists and open-source thinkers came together to explore a simple but radical idea – that improvements in agriculture could be achieved by reducing barriers to knowledge exchange. They were convinced that transforming agricultural technology into a shared endeavour would result in an adaptive, open and resilient food system, reflecting the values of the grower and the larger community.

Farm Hack began as an ambitious voluntary project between technologists and agriculturalists. The National Young Farmers Coalition started a blog called 'Farm Hack', launching the first programme, and they were later joined by maker/hacker networks. The community expanded across America through online and in-person social networks. Farm Hack is now a rapidly growing repository of agricultural knowledge, with thousands of active members, containing numerous open designs and documentation for farming technologies and practices. The basic idea is that 'agriculture is a shared human endeavour'.

Farm Hack is a culture of collaborative problem solving. On most farms, identifying problems and testing solutions (003ES/FH/03), then assessing them, is a daily practice. Within its first year, the Farm Hack website featured documentation for over 100 innovative agricultural tools (003ES/FH/01) – ranging from manufacturing instructions for farm-built hardware such as garlic planters, to the remanufacturing of 'extinct' farm-scale equipment (003ES/FH/04). Dorn Cox, one of Farm Hack's founders, offered his advice: 'I've been able to see the regeneration and open-source or open-knowledge exchange really shift as far as its cultural acceptance [goes] in the last five years ... organizations like GODAN (the Global Open Data for Agriculture and Nutrition) are coming together saying, "We need to be sharing open-source data and open-source platforms." [We] are still a spark rather than a flame, but it seems that as an

idea it is spreading. It's part of an underlying global culture recognizing the need for more individual local control ... [We struggle with] the balance between scaling up ... and creating an authentic community that is peer-to-peer driven and not in the model of a lot of traditional NGOs. The quality and pace of ... development is slower because it isn't what contributors do exclusively.' Funding changed the relationship between paid workers and volunteers: 'The quality of the platform improved, but the quality of the dialogue diminished ... [We went] from an organization of a core group of volunteers that put on lots of events ourselves to recognizing that to scale the traditional way would have meant raising a lot of money and creating an organization to be able to host and provide international chapters. Ideas are important and instigating local in-person events are critical, because people take it upon themselves. That's both a strength and a weakness, because it's less of an organization and more of an idea ... For example, when we started we were small, [and] forums worked because of that. Our online platform doesn't reflect the larger community and how they interact ... [We] try to support our community by following our design principles of findable, accessible, interoperable, reusable, inexpensive, interoperable, accessible, replicable, repairable and modular ... [Farm Hack as a] concept and platform is nowhere near perfect, but we've thought through many of the elements of documentation and exchange ... We're still in a prototype phase.'

Cox said that is an 'experiment to develop a platform to document and exchange the ideas as a reflection of our local environment with the understanding that those ideas can be globally shared but locally adapted, and that fundamental to democratic tools and democratic living is that people have the ability to create and own tools to improve their environment.' They take time over their operational and organizational structure, and they have inspirational vision (003ES/FH/02). They align brilliant talent and capability with clear briefs that have impact. Meanwhile, different tools and platforms are emerging: 'Farm Hack is one piece of the larger experiment in regenerative economies and agricultural knowledge exchange.' They help contributors leave their own circles, giving them international context and reach.

+

004 ACC
ES
SIBL
DES
IG

004
ACCESSIBLE DESIGN

E

N

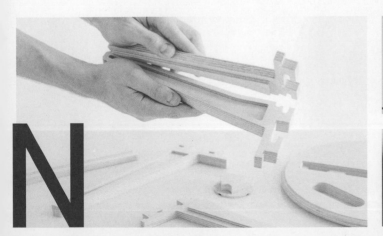

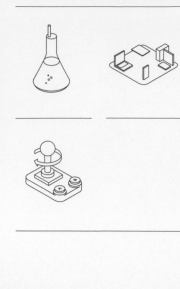

+ 004AD/K/01

Taking a traditional
craft and enabling
audiences

KNITERATE

+ 004AD/K/02

Knitting – once the preserve of grannies, in recent times undertaken by hipsters – is now a vehicle for large distribution. Kniterate is a digital knitting machine that can transform our relationship with clothing, using yarn to 'print' digital clothing files (004AD/K/01). Enabled by an internet platform, users can design garments, edit templates or upload personal images for output. Knitting machines range from rudimentary boards with pegs to totally automated and computerized devices. Kniterate has hundreds of computer-controlled needles to create loops, which combine to create knitwear. These can be ready to use, like scarves and beanies, or require further assembly, like a sweater. Standard clothing sizes have always been a law unto themselves; this enables truly bespoke sizing. Personalized goods provide new revenue streams through brand loyalty, in a time of increasing buyer sophistication (004AD/K/02).

Kniterate is a tool that makes bespoke creation affordable for both consumers and makers. The company's intention is to change the garment industry's supply chain model. Currently retailers ship garments internationally, resulting in excess stock that they are forced to mark down or even throw away. Kniterate enables clothing to be made locally, on demand, without waste from cutting fabrics. It also helps fashion designers avoid the long lead-times associated with the outsourcing of testing and manufacturing designs, and provides a tool for makers to experiment with. This will accelerate innovation in parallel ways, comparable to electronic component access, which led to garage hackers creating personal computers. Adding to this movement towards distributed manufacturing, Kniterate has created an easy-to-use version of an industrial knitting machine that can be installed in workshops, at ten times lower cost than industrial peers.

Co-founder Gerard Rubio shared his insights into the publicly engaged design of knitted goods. '[I] always loved mechanical stuff and taking things apart to understand how they work, and knitting machines were very interesting. They're complicated, with lots of moving parts. They are fascinating, but there was something wrong. In the 21st century, people were using these machines with punch cards and running them manually. I thought this should be automated: with 3D printing you can design your file and then send it to machines to make it for you. A eureka moment occurred: "Why not do the same for clothing? Have the same machine that allows you to go from a digital file into a final garment?"'

Rubio said of their two-stage interconnected mission: 'The first one is empowering small businesses. We're offering a semi-industrial machine for people to scale up their production, companies that do a lot of manual work, and they are limited because they have only two hands or are maybe hiring people, two or three more, a few more pieces, but still it's a lot of labour. By providing a machine that automates the process they'll be able to grow a little more. At the same time, [we're] trying to educate society about technology, this concept of locally manufactured clothing.'

SUGRU

Building a community
that understands the
application better
than you do

+ 004AD/S/01

+ + ## Sugru has the same reach as Sellotape or Post-It Notes because its uses are so broad.

+ 004AD/S/02

+ 004AD/S/03

Anyone who has been to a 'make-a-thon', 'hackathon' or design sprint will be familiar with this hand-mouldable magic material that turns into strong, flexible rubber overnight. Once cured, Sugru is waterproof (004AD/S/02), just like other rubbers. You can use it in the shower, the sink or even the sea. It's a material that you can take anywhere, and was invented for people to repair and improve products – with infinite possibilities. It enables people to fix more and throw away less, from homeowners through to people making small gadgets and even toys. Sugru sticks to many materials, forming a strong bond with aluminium, steel, ceramics, glass, wood and other materials, including some plastics and rubbers. Sugru's durable cured properties mean it will stay strong and securely bonded anywhere from the freezer to a hot shower, and from the garden to the great outdoors.

Jane Ní Dhulchaointigh is the inventor and CEO of Sugru. She studied at the Royal College of Art in London, where she had an idea that led to the first version of Sugru in 2003. One of her experiments, during her Master's degree in Design Products, was to combine bathroom sealant with wood dust. It made balls that bounced when dropped. 'It was just a surprising moment. I made something that looked like wood and it bounced,' she said. 'I just wanted to create something that looked interesting or behaved in an interesting way, which could then lead me somewhere else.' Ní Dhulchaointigh's lightbulb moment came while she was washing up and struggling with a leaking plug that was causing water to drain

away. So she took her sealant and hand moulded it around the plug for a temporary fix. She then saw that a substance to enable easy repairs or even improvements to everyday products would fulfil a need. Six years and 8,000 lab hours later, the formula for Sugru was complete.

Sugru launched in December 2009 and its community of users has continued to grow, with 10 million mini-packs reaching people in over 160 countries worldwide. Ní Dhulchaointigh is passionate about promoting a creative culture of resourcefulness, and wants to change our systemic throwaway mindset. The project has become not just about the material, but also about creating a community that can 'fix' and transform things to meet personal requirements. Sugru is a very marketable product as it is so adaptable and pliable, and empowers the user. The organization has a track record of raising vast capital quickly; for example, they raised £3.5 million through crowdfunding. This broke their original £1 million target in four days. The largest single investment was £1 million, and they now have shareholders in 68 countries.

Sugru's most important lesson is their process of putting people first. Since their creation, they have used their blog to publish users' applications for their material. This simple media tool not only tested the material, but grew a community and demonstrated creative uses that people could identify with, calling them 'stories'. On the blog, published applications have included: wheelchair repair, washing machine restoration, computer cable holders with Lego, bespoke bike adaptions, fixing

OPPOSITE:
+ 004AD/S/04

+ FUTUREKIND
+ 004 ACCESSIBLE DESIGN

+ SUGRU

+ 137

+ 004AD/S/05

broken toys and mending laptop chargers. The stories are all accessible and curated, but really allow people to understand how they could use the material (004AD/S/05). The more personal stories include empowering family members, for example: 'Our grandad was struggling to pick up and answer his phone, so my sister Sugru-ed it! Now it's raised off the table so he can pick it up, and the main button he needs has been raised too, so he can answer calls easily without fumbling.'

Sugru is providing a means of social technology, as it is actively encouraging repairing of items, thus making products last longer (004AD/S/04). Currently, in Sweden, the government is exploring tax breaks for repairing products. This empowers people and changes the relationship they have with objects and products in their home. Sugru is taking that approach into people's homes, building a bridge that enables people to make repairs. The negative side of encouraging repair is that success depends on the contextual situation that surrounds that repair, and quality control. There is also the potential for uninformed users to hurt themselves or others around them ... for example, if someone repairs a friend's bike and they have an accident, who is liable? But perhaps ideally we should all just learn to be adults bound by our capabilities, and seek advice where appropriate – or be bold?

Sugru has received recognition from *Time* magazine as one of the '50 Best Inventions of 2010', and has been dubbed the '21st century duct tape' by Forbes. In 2012,

Ní Dhulchaointigh won the inaugural London Design Festival Design Entrepreneur award. Sugru's most recent accolades include 'Best DIY Product' (2015), awarded by the British Hardware Federation, who described it as 'a great household solution'. The annual DIY Week Awards ceremony agreed that Sugru is a 'truly innovative and exciting product'.

+ + Products are designed to suit as many people as possible rather than the needs of the individual.

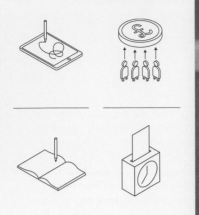

+ 004AD/A/01

Redesigning prosthetics
for young children with
a global perspective

AMBIONICS

+ 004AD/A/02

Sol Smith-Ryan had his arm amputated after his birth, due to a blood clot. His father, Ben Ryan, wanted him to have a prosthetic limb urgently, but was told they did not exist for infants under three. Unsatisfied with the NHS options, the psychology teacher began fabricating a bionic arm for his son, using accessible CAD software. His solution has transformed the lead-time of three months to cast and build a fibreglass prosthetic, to having a printed version ready in a matter of days. It has opened up a new world of opportunities for the family and medical care delivery. Ben quit his day job to concentrate on prosthetics full-time, setting up Ambionics. Their core mission is 'to create cutting-edge prosthetic products that deliver innovative design and empower people to live more engaging lives (004AD/A/01)'. In interview, Ryan shared his insights.

'[Sol] was born in an awkward position, with a forceps injury to his left arm. There was considerable pressure from the hospital to remove all of the bones below the humerus, everything south of the elbow, even though there was a possibility of saving a very small amount ... [Five weeks later] I wanted to intervene and try to offer Sol some kind of prosthetic. I started when he was lying on his back, underneath a hoop, with toys suspended on it ... [I] was lowering toys so that he could reach them with his short arm, five weeks after he'd come home from having an amputation. At that point I realized I'm modifying the wrong thing. I extended his reach, for less than a pound, by using a kitchen sponge and a piece of bandage, which were taped onto his little arm, and he instantly started playing with both toys ... [The biggest challenge is the] fatty tissue with babies; it's very difficult to get an electrical impulse under the age of three. I had to try and find a way of bridging that gap, and that's really where the project came from: me filling a need that hasn't been met worldwide.'

Ryan defines social technology as a process: 'Rather than applying design principles to a problem, [you need to] actually look at the problem and really understand it before you make any decisions – so take a bottom-up approach and address needs first, without compromise. I also see that there is a natural marriage between engineering and psychology

that's quite rare. Most of my engineering and design decisions are informed by psychology, helping me to address my own son's needs.'

Ryan's repeatable insights can encourage us all to '[keep] things as simple as they need to be. I'm specifically trying to work with children [from] eight months of age, so as soon as they can sit up, until about three. There are already products out there for children who have had a successful intervention and who have gone [on] to accept prosthetics. There's plenty out there from the age of three onwards, but there was nothing for children under the age of three; everything seemed to have been over-engineered. There were too many small parts and complicated fixtures and fittings that just meant that the devices were not safe for the children and the age group that needed them.' The interesting link between psychology and design was highlighted to Ryan: 'If a child hasn't got a functional grasp by the end of the first period of brain pruning, which is where the brain eliminates nerves that are not needed (the noise in the brain); if children haven't learned to master a prosthetic that grabs by the age of two-and-a-half, they will disengage with prosthetics, only to re-engage in the self-conscious teen years. What I'm trying to do is bridge that gap by just simplifying things. You don't need five articulated fingers to hold a book steady; you just need a small, movable thumb. It doesn't need to have tendons and complex joints; just by applying pressure under the armpit, Sol will be able to hold the corner of a book simply and reliably.'

Ryan foresees that the uptake of cheaper accessible scanning technologies will transform this industry. 'At the moment, I'm working on a beta trial with families in every continent. I'm trialling a process of them using really, really cheap gaming technology – Xbox Kinect scanners – to scan their children's limbs while they're asleep, [and] send me a file. I will then produce a prosthetic socket and mail it to them, wherever they are in the world. I would personally like to see them regarded more as we regard shoes for our children (004AD/A/02). It would be very easy to get the wrong size shoe for your child and cause calluses and all sorts of things.'

WIKI HOUSE

Empowering people to
create downloadable
homes through
a platform

OPPOSITE:
+ 004AD/WH/02

+ 004AD/WH/01

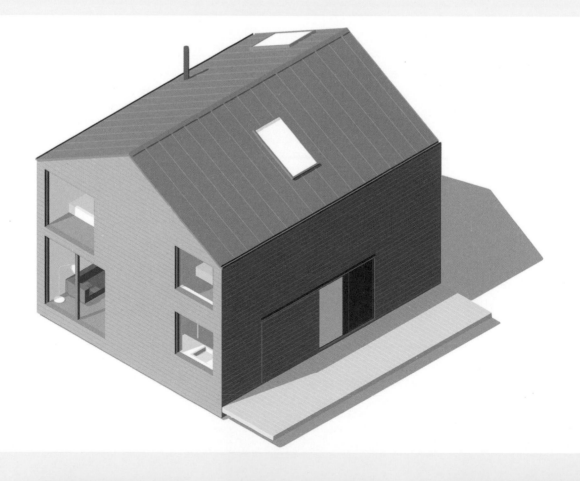

+ + Designers have a fantastic skill for creating unified interfaces for everything: it is just speaking to the people.

+ 004AD/WH/03

WikiHouse is an open-source construction set; anyone can design, download and 'print' houses and components, intended to be assembled with minimal skills or training (004AD/WH/01). The components can be digitally manufactured in centralized factories, but also by a distributed network of small businesses and maker spaces. Anyone can 'print' and assemble plans for under £50,000 (004AD/WH/03). A studio costs under £15,000, a micro house under £50,000, and a townhouse around £130,000. The aim is to build digital tools, unlocking a new, sustainable, resilient and scalable housing industry (004AD/WH/02). This will make housing development more affordable, democratic, circular and sustainable. WikiHouse is a collaborative R&D project being developed by a consortium of world-leading companies, organizations, government representatives and funders to build a shared infrastructure and open standards for the digital housing economy. First, users choose their design and download free plans, then send the plans to a sawmill where shaped components are cut from sheet material, such as plywood, by a CNC machine. The pieces are delivered to site for user assembly. Similar to IKEA flat-pack furniture, the kit contains everything to build the house (004AD/WH/06), including make-your-own tools such as a mallet and ladder. As an open-source

project (004AD/WH/04), the WikiHouse idea has spread internationally. WikiHouses have been built in Christchurch, New Zealand, as a response to earthquakes, and aid agencies are reviewing using WikiHouse for disaster relief.

Justyna Swat is a strategic designer who encourages design for social impact through interdisciplinary approaches, advocating for people to look at the bigger picture in order to answer the right questions. Swat is a founder of POC21 and is active in Fab Cities. Her WikiHouse role promotes social engagement, as she explained in an interview: '[WikiHouse] came from an architectural office called 00, with the question "What's the proof of concept of distributed manufacturing?" The exhibition was done on CNC machines, so there was plywood and machines. It was not thought to be a project that was going to change the world, but was an example of distributed manufacturing.' When questioned about the lessons they would impart to others Swat responded: 'Build a community. A very important thing is never start [blind] – if you want to start something, always look [to see] if there is someone else already doing it. If you do social design, look at who is the closest already existing community, and how can you build up and help them out; that's one thing. Then, once you do it, when you get the

+ + There is the WikiHouse construction system and the WikiHouse Foundation, which is an umbrella overseeing all the local chapters of WikiHouse, plus the development of a platform.

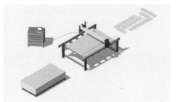

+ 004AD/WH/04

+ 004AD/WH/05

community that's doing something, never think that, because you have a different background, or because they're doctors and you're – I don't know, an architect or a designer – then maybe you won't have anything to do with them.'

'[Make sure you find] the most opposite, because you might bring skills that they don't have, and that might be exciting for them actually. The community [is about] finding, not starting, a new thing. It is something that's sort of a transition. It's going to require a transition phase. Maybe start by meet-ups and things, and then once you find your community, slowly transition, if it's actively just doing social design, because that sometimes doesn't pay. When someone is really passionate and an activist, you're going to meet at the beginning the fact of not being well paid, so that's going to require transitioning.'

The most important element of these types of initiative is how they become financially sustainable. WikiHouse 'believe that if you design for social impact, it has to have an economical case … Try to make sure that there is a need for what you're designing. I mean don't design useless things. I've nothing against art, and I think it's super-important, but I think we have to dissociate those two things. If you're

designing for social impact, make sure that what you're designing is really needed. If it's needed, there is an economy for that; or, if it's not there, it's going to be soon. Yes, make sure that what you're designing has a user (004AD/WH/07). If it has the user, there's going to be an economy for that, so it's going to slowly move from the NGO.' When asked what we should all be designing for, 'energy' was WikiHouse's clear response. 'We have all signed to say that we're going to reduce our carbon footprint. There are so many energy sources that are commonly known; solar panels, wind, etc. I truly believe in the centralization of energy production. It is a topic that's complex and technical, and there are many solutions that are there, but they're just not user-friendly. People are looking into that, but they consider DIY, and not everyone wants to do DIY.'

+ 004AD/WH/06

+ 004AD/WH/07

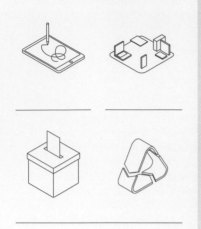

+ 004AD/OS/01

Design for collaboration,
interoperability,
interconnection,
disassembly – and
spare parts

OPEN
STRUCTURES

+ 004AD/OS/02

OpenStructures is a modular construction platform that uses a shared geometrical grid, where 'everyone designs for everyone'. It enables users to create their own individual objects, trade and/or collaborate. The project works to define a three-dimensional open-source code for common hardware and the built environment. It initiates a 'collaborative Meccano' to which everybody can contribute parts, components and structures (004AD/OS/01).

Its founder, Thomas Lommee, commented: 'The purpose of this experiment is to investigate what the opportunities and limitations of an open modular system are, and under which conditions it will prove to be most efficient and favourable.' The OpenStructures platform offers a universal process with interoperable constraints, leading to the unboxing of products, and increases their repairability (004AD/OS/02). OpenStructures offers a universal language for people who design and fabricate objects, ultimately leading to a cleaner, faster user experience. The projects goal is to initiate a collective 'Lego-like' structure to be utilized by anyone, from large manufacturers to remote craftsmen. OpenStructures is underpinned by a 'components database', enabling users to upload, review components, trade, and build universal 'bills of materials' in a shared space.

In interview Lommee clarified their start point, lessons and valuable insights: '[The backstory was] redesigning the way products are made; how they are sold, used and how they eventually are reused and recycled and so on. Modularity allows for much more flexibility within design, and also allows for the object, or for the design – whether it's an object or a house or a built environment – to evolve along with the user ... [I wanted] to look into what the basic principles are that just seem to work. If I would take ancient principles and

++ OpenStructures is a design script that generates non-intimidating objects, where even somebody with little affinity for repairing or taking things apart is stimulated to try it.

+ + Using their hardware library, users can build their own spare parts, ending the perennial cycle of buying and trashing appliances.

Grinder

A. Adaptor - 3D Printed
OpenStructures Compatible
thingiverse.com/thing:25794

B. Switch Cover - 3D Printed
OpenStructures Compatible
thingiverse.com/thing:25793

C. Plastic Housing
Vacuum Formed
protospace.nl/formech-660

D. Stainless Steel Blade
Hand Made
1.5 mm stainless steel plate

E. AC Motor
Recuperated
from Bodum 5679 or similar

F. Glass Jar
Recuperated
70mm lid size

G. Toggle Switch
Standard Component
rs-online.com / item#734-7141

H. M4 Bolts
Standard Component

I. M4 Lock Nut
Standard Component

J. M3 Bolts
Standard Component

+ 004AD/OS/03

bring them into the present with context and the current infrastructure, both physical and digital, how would that look? Very quickly there was a merge between modularity and open source, the idea that one bigger system is not developed by one entity, but actually by a lot of small contributions by a lot of entities.'

'OpenStructures is a design script that generates and produces non-intimidating objects, where even somebody who maybe [has] no affinity with repairing, adapting or taking things apart is stimulated to try it anyway due to simplicity. It's lowering the threshold to again start to repair and start to adapt yourself, and even start to produce things, and it's also allowing for encounters and dialogue and working together (004AD/OS/03) ... [The project wanted to address a] common design language [that] could start to make links between users and between industry and consumers and retailers. It was just a very challenging thought. At that moment there was also a lot happening around open-source development, especially within the digital realm, seeing the first 3D printers popping up with all these other platforms like crowdfunding platforms, etc. ... giving oxygen to this idea.'

OpenStructures understood that 'it was actually not just about the ecological aspect, about facilitating the reuse of components and facilitating recycling by designing for disassembly. This open-source development of things was coming from dialogue happening between all the different contributors ... [We] thought this project would spread

from the outside in, that [we] would set up a platform and, like Wikipedia or Airbnb, people would pick it up and it would just go global in no time and I would receive interesting parts from various corners of the world and it would all fit.' However, actually the community required building, showing them the capability and opportunity, and placing a lot of value on engagement.

When questioned about their lessons, OpenStructures highlighted the importance of depth of study, passion and enjoyment (004AD/OS/04). '[It is very] important that you really develop things ... Every moment that you stop, and you think about "Am I still enjoying this, and is this really something that works for me? Doing this project, is it making my life better, or is it generating fulfilling experiences?" It's important not to try to push things too quickly, just to take your time and to observe and to do it, to make prototypes, to really test it, constantly test and re-test and re-evaluate and try to develop it like that, but not try to rush. It should be fun, that's essential ... [This] project still really needs this face-to-face interaction in this very physical component of being able to hold things, understand things, configure them, take them apart; this is a very important aspect of the project (004AD/OS/05). Ultimately, the whole essence of this project is not about the object or maybe not even about the space, but it's really about what it generates, what it facilitates and what it makes possible again.'

+ 004AD/OS/04

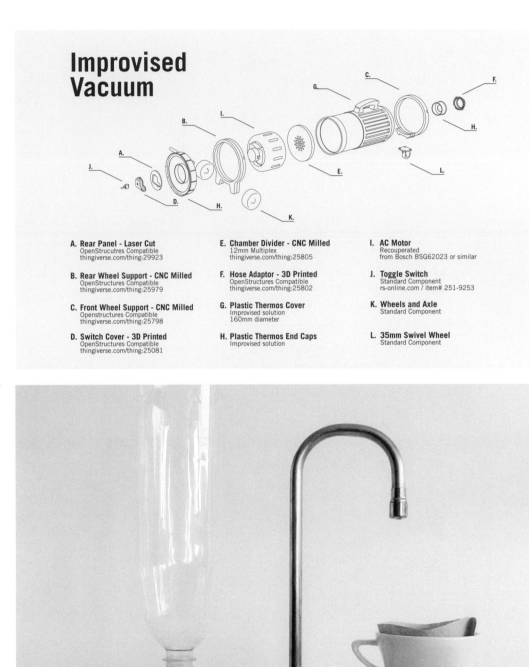

Improvised Vacuum

A. Rear Panel - Laser Cut
OpenStrucutres Compatible
thingiverse.com/thing:29923

B. Rear Wheel Support - CNC Milled
OpenStructures Compatible
thingiverse.com/thing:25979

C. Front Wheel Support - CNC Milled
Openstructures Compatible
thingiverse.com/thing:25798

D. Switch Cover - 3D Printed
OpenStructures Compatible
thingiverse.com/thing:25081

E. Chamber Divider - CNC Milled
12mm Multiplex
thingiverse.com/thing:25805

F. Hose Adaptor - 3D Printed
OpenStructures Compatible
thingiverse.com/thing:25802

G. Plastic Thermos Cover
Improvised solution
160mm diameter

H. Plastic Thermos End Caps
Improvised solution

I. AC Motor
Recouperated
from Bosch BSG62023 or similar

J. Toggle Switch
Standard Component
rs-online.com / item# 251-9253

K. Wheels and Axle
Standard Component

L. 35mm Swivel Wheel
Standard Component

+ 004AD/OS/05

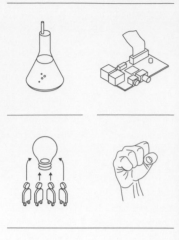

+ 004AD/SC/01

SAFECAST

+ 004AD/SC/02

+ 004AD/SC/03

+ 004AD/SC/04

The Fukushima Daiichi nuclear power plant disaster tore a hole in lives, communities and the surrounding environment, following reactor damage after a catastrophic earthquake and tsunami. The events forced 160,000 people to flee their homes. The nuclear disaster initiated the closure of all of Japan's 44 working reactors, responsible for producing a third of the national energy output, and resulted in mainland radioactive contamination. One day after this incident, Safecast, a volunteer organization monitoring and sharing information on environmental radiation, was born (004AD/SC/01).

The project started with Joi Ito, MIT Media Lab director, and Pieter Franken discussing which Geiger counters residents could obtain in Fukushima, and realizing that nothing was accessible to the general population. Their role was to aid the collation, aggregation and dissemination of radiation data. The initial capital of US$37,000 was crowdfunded in 30 days. Initial unit costs were US$450, reducing over time with larger production volumes. Safecast is now a volunteer organization devoted to providing a science-centred radiation mapping solution (004AD/SC/02). After the nuclear incident, accurate and trustworthy radiation information was publicly unavailable. Safecast has enabled people to easily monitor their own homes and environments, freeing themselves from dependency on the government and other institutions for this essential information.

The founding members started wanting to aggregate publicly available Japanese radiation data, using accessible online maps. Their first systems included units fitted to cars, drones, bikes and people; now they build kits so that anyone can upload data, empowering the masses. Care has been taken to develop hardware and software systems, nurturing the growth of a community that is attractive to worldwide citizen scientists, encouraging participation. Not surprisingly, different technical skill sets are required in the community – from data visualization to people who want to check radiation levels on online maps. The entire project has been designed to be intuitive for poorly informed citizens, who are the primary drivers of the whole system.

Safecast create data-gathering units while running community-led workshops, assisting software development, developing hardware and analysing data published under Creative Commons protocols. Volunteer data contributors choose worthwhile locations for data gathering. Post-submission arbiters confirm data quality and approve it for database inclusion. For decades, conventional radiation-monitoring involved a small number of certified experts conducting measurements using expensive and sensitive detectors. The alternative risked scaremongering as a result of incorrect data, manipulation or over-zealous reporting. At some point, however, grassroots technical systems need to be seen for what they are: opportunities for communities to empower themselves with the deployment of hundreds of low-cost detectors of identical design (004AD/SC/03). Leading experts believe that, with correct training and oversight, volunteers can collect data equal to that collected by experts.

Key principles include crowdsourcing, and open-source, open-data and information commons, showing the benefits of transparency. Safecast's goal is to assemble a database of observations. The achievement of social outcomes, promoting openness, was an original motivation supported by an ad-hoc voluntary structure, embodying a collaborative culture. Safecast believe in openness and transparency, with the use of open-source hardware and software considered essential. All designs are publicly available for scrutiny, enabling outside observers to evaluate the tools and methodology.

Open-data publication principles accompany this community response approach. The information and ability to get that data did not exist, so the team depended on experts for success at first. Some of the relationships were created through location; however, finding motivated participants is critical. The project bucks a trend of locational expertise and places the capability in the hands of the general public. The largest challenge is finances; the project is privately funded and also relies on donations. This project is about community empowerment, and not just profit margins. Safecast opens the debate of information accessibility, arming people with the power to call government bodies to action.

+ 004AD/PP/01

Redesigning waste
harvesting

PRECIOUS PLASTICS

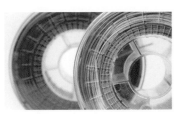

+ 004AD/PP/02

Precious Plastics' goal is to develop the ultimate plastics recycling machinery and share open-source plans online. Last year the world produced nearly 311 million tonnes of plastic, with less than 10% being recycled. Most plastic detritus ends up in landfills and oceans, or inside animals. However, Precious Plastics propose a solution to this 'plastic problem'. They want to empower people internationally to download designs and build machines, and to start locally productive, plastic recycling centres (004AD/PP/02). In these centres, local plastic waste is collected and transformed, turning it into new products or opportunities (004AD/PP/01). The machine parts are sourced from scrapyards and fashioned into three units that manipulate plastic trash.

Each machine uses different methods: 1) a rotational moulding device, 2) an extrusion machine and 3) an injection-moulding machine along with a shredder. The rotation machine is actually a rotational oven, heating the plastic to form hollow objects. Extrusion is often used for extruding lines and pipes. Meanwhile, most of our plastic products are made with the extrusion technique, which is usually quick and efficient. Precious Plastics' founder, Dave Hakkens, doesn't envision these machines as consumer products but rather as being used in small communities where people can be reimbursed for their plastic waste and provided with opportunities to make saleable outputs. The blueprints for the inventions enable others to expand the range of products and refine the machines. In interview, Hakkens shared his insights.

'[Our] mission is to recycle more plastic, because it's a functional material; we use it so inefficiently, because we throw it away, burn it and it hurts our environment. We would be more effective with it; we could create closed-loop systems with it, and not

+ + Precious Plastics want to empower people globally to download designs and build machines, and to start locally productive plastic recycling centres.

+ 004AD/PP/03

+ 004AD/PP/04

+ + It's better if we all execute a small solution and bring it all together. Problems are not solved by one person ... but by communities either online or in the world.

+ 004AD/PP/05

waste it ... [We jumped] into this research project as it's complex for the industry to recycle on a large scale, so they prefer to buy new material. We should provide people with tools and machines so they can work with plastic (004AD/PP/04). Just like people work with wood and metal on a smaller scale, I wanted to enable them to work with plastic on a smaller scale, to start recycling in their own neighbourhood ... [In] this type of work we tend to pay a lot of attention to numbers, to views or to counts or to statistics, but I noticed that Precious Plastics really hit the people it needed. For me that was a super-valuable lesson in [terms of] "don't pay too much attention to the internet".'

The insights Hakkens would offer are, first, 'Don't be overwhelmed by the problems in the world, and realistically do the things you can. There are many ways to solve a problem, [and] people get stuck in having the best solution, but not knowing how to execute it. It's better if we all execute a small solution and bring it all together. Problems are not solved by one person; [they're] solved by communities either online or in the world. Dive into something, do as much research as you can, and start working on it and share what you do so others can build up on your ideas and your suggestions ... [It is] easier to communicate your potential solution or design with the world and bring people together to all work on specific topics. It's powerful what designers can do, they can make complex ideas visible and understandable so people can understand and participate. As a tool set,

that's a powerful thing to learn, to execute your ideas and bring people together.'

'[I] really like this ecosystem around plastic recycling, that our machines do not require building and shipping internationally, you have these local areas where people start. Some guys in Spain have made a water filter you put on an old glass jar, from recycled plastic ... [All] my projects are open source, it is an effective way of sharing ideas with the world. I don't think everything needs to be open source, it's a way of tackling problems. It's important to review your skills, and how you can contribute. In the end all those things together make your combination unique, and so valuable to the world ... [I] like to work in these complex global problems, and I think as an individual they tend to look too complex for one person, they look overwhelming to start on. It often seems like you don't have enough resources or money or people to do something about it, like you need a huge organization to make a change. I always liked the manoeuvre between those two elements; you don't need a huge amount of resources, but just as an individual or a few individuals. Using the power of the internet you can still make quite some change or improvements. The thing is in this world [there are] a lot of opportunities, as a small group of people can have the most impact.'

FIELD READY

Redesigning humanitarian opportunities with local manufacturing

+ 004AD/FR/01

+ 004AD/FR/02

Field Ready is a non-profit humanitarian organization, filling a gap in the delivery of international aid (004AD/FR/01). Their vision is guided by transforming how needs are met and assets/capabilities are created and built. Their concept transforms logistics through technology, innovative design and participation, bringing manufacturing to challenging places, and training others to solve health, water and sanitation problems locally. They scale their approach to each scenario, dramatically improving efficiency in aid delivery, and reducing costs, transport needs and time. They use 3D printers, laser cutters and traditional manufacturing, and share skills through training. Their approach is about mutual respect, openness to learning, experimentation and engaging a wide range of stakeholders.

Their principles include: 1) Professionalism – they operate in a financially sustainable manner to promote effective programmes, positive change and learning. 2) Appropriateness – they effectively develop products and services that are practical for people in need, including those working in response. 3) Partnership – the enormous challenges faced in humanitarian contexts require a unified approach, so they work in close cooperation with others sharing mutual goals. 4) Adherence to humanitarian principles, including humanity, independence and impartiality. Field Ready's mission is international aid development through access to goods 'where they need them and when they need them'. They achieve international impact through free and open sharing of reliable designs for essential humanitarian supplies, a strong community of expert designers and engineers to support local people with custom design assistance, and robust manufacturing equipment suitable for field use that is repairable and maintainable. Dr Eric James, the co-founder, shared his inspirational insights.

'Humanitarian supply chains account for a huge portion of development assistance that goes overseas. Up to 70% of humanitarian aid is devoted to logistics. If we can reduce that, we're talking about a major cost saving, so making things far cheaper than they currently are; we're talking about doing it far faster, because if we're making things where they're needed it can be done, in some cases, in just a number of hours … Because we're able to pass on skills to people locally they can do repairs and actually reach mass production without relying on long processes … [Impactful examples have included] babies in Haiti missing umbilical cord clamps, [being] forced to use things like discarded shoelaces that can be contaminated, leading to sepsis; resulting in increased child morbidity and mortality.'

The second example involves rudimentary technology 'in the worst humanitarian crisis we've faced since the Second World War, the Syrian Civil War. We know about bombs being dropped on cities, collapsed buildings and people rescued from rubble. Rescue teams were under-equipped, and rescue equipment can be very expensive; a good way to lift slabs of concrete didn't exist. Usually you only need to lift them a few inches … to be able to pull people out. There is equipment that does that costing up to $5,000 … [Field Ready found a British standard for] rescue airbags – and created a process to make them at a tenth of the cost in Syria (004AD/FR/02). The project was first used to rescue a mother and daughter and is now being distributed to rescue teams in Syria.'

James said that 'you have to start with a clear identification of what problems – singular or plural – you're going to work on, and that requires refinement and its communication. A second insight is bringing in or making a strong team. We're not all aid workers, we're not all engineers … that would've led to a certain thing. We have a designer, a large set of diverse engineers, people with different experiences. We're aid workers with management experience and commercial start-up experience, etc.'

Finally, he advised: 'Design and create processes to get out of the building. In the 20-plus years I've been doing this work, [we couldn't have foreseen] the idea 20 years ago that all refugees would be talking to themselves on mobile phones that then were connected to the internet … You have to get outside of the box and think about things like post-normal times. This is what we're doing with Field Ready: it's not about what we can do today, it's about what we can do in the future with it, and how we can shape that for a social good that's so important.'

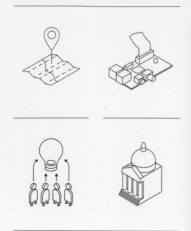

+ 004AD/OWP/01

Democratizing
knowledge through
community
engagement

OPEN
WATER
PROJECT

+ 004AD/OWP/02

Session Two:
Building and Using a DIY
Water Conductivity Sensor

Duration:
2 hours

Materials Needed: Class Preparation:

1. Three plastic or paper cups for each group   1. Assemble one Coqui to use as a demo
2. One bottle of mineral water (Pellegrino, Evian,   unit
   Perrier)   2. Download the Introduction to
3. Several black permanent markers for labeling   Measuring Water Quality Powerpoint from
   the cups   http://bit.ly/MeasuringWaterConductivity
4. One Coqui kit for every group   3. Pull up the Coqui Beginner's Tutorial in
                                                    a web browser (http://bit.ly/CoquiTutorial)

Homework to assign to students prior to session:

1. Collect water samples as detailed in Session 1 along with a photograph of each location
2. Ask students to write down the location of each sample.

Coqui:

The Coqui is an educational
water conductivity sensor
designed by Don Blair and
Public Lab. The Coqui makes a
higher frequency sound when
it senses higher conductivity
and a lower frequency sound
for lower conductivity. The
name 'coqui' comes from the
common name for several
species of frogs that live in
Puerto Rico and make the
sound 'coqui, coqui' at night.

+ 004AD/OWP/03

The Open Water Project develops low-cost, open-source tools that enable communities to collect, interpret and share water-quality data. Traditional water monitoring is expensive, often preventing homeowners from testing well-water quality. The project's low-cost hardware devices measure common water-quality parameters, using DIY materials and designs for anyone to build, modify and deploy water-quality sensors in their neighbourhood (004AD/OWP/01). Measured data includes temperature, conductivity, depth and turbidity. They encourage community growth focused on 'free and open' approaches to water science (004AD/OWP/02), supporting ongoing work by grassroots parties interested in personal water quality. In an interview, Catherine D'Ignazio – one of the co-founders of the Open Water Project, along with Don Blair and others – shared her insights.

'[The mission was to] reduce the cost of continuous water measurement (004AD/OWP/03). So, our question was, how do you engage more people in the process beyond the usual professional suspects? We consulted with professionals and scientists along the way while continually editing the process … making it cheaper and more accessible, providing some guidance and community around this idea of water collection. We continually seek to answer the question "How might we bring more people and voices into this process and stimulate public dialogue?"'

'One of the most exciting things has been the conversations through our meet-ups, where we convene a lot of different kinds of stakeholders. We had people who were professional scientists, environmental advocates, hackers and citizen groups. There's a lot of environmental justice advocacy and activism along the Mystic River in Boston because it's a very industrial site and very contaminated. Participants were advocating for clean water, and they were excited about having a cheap way to measure these things, to take and show to officials in charge or send to a court. There were these nexuses of people that had not previously talked to each other. Finally, for me as an educator, I took the circuit into my journalism classroom, using it as a teaching tool to say "on the one hand, this is not that hard, journalism students in half an hour can build this circuit from

scratch and stick it in water". It questioned the role of the storyteller and the producer of media and information if they can go about and monitor their own rivers and lakes in their cities looking for contaminants themselves.' When asked about their repeatable lessons, D'Ignazio commented: 'Think about how your process is your product. Product people and technologists often think that what they're doing is building technology; frequently the most valuable thing you're building is the community. You're building connections between people that would otherwise not be connecting, and the technology or the thing that you're making becomes an excuse – all being well a good one – and hopefully you do build something that is useful in the world. But often those conversations can be the seed of other kinds of collaborations and then produce other kinds of communities that go forwards … [Secondly] don't put all your eggs in the product basket – like, we just need to produce this one thing and then everyone's going to come and use it. Well, because you haven't produced the community, it doesn't come out of an authentic process; where you engaged people that care about this thing in the world you have to go and find them and gather their input.'

'There is a tension in citizen science: "Is the data good enough, and good enough for who?" And that caused a lot of internal tension … people who were working on this project had different views about that. On the one hand, "It's not really science if we can't make it truly accurate," [and] on the other, "It may be good enough for certain purposes." The lessons I've learned are the aspirations that we have for volunteer-run, crowdsourced, citizen-science group projects. We need to think about the mechanism for supporting these ad-hoc volunteers. Ultimately, we did have some infrastructure from the Public Lab as an organization, so they have staff and support to keep community conversations going online, but then the project was never formally funded, making it dependent on who had free time. You could have a more deliberate design process with more resources, involving more diverse people. [And this is why] we can't place all our eggs in the basket of volunteer-run citizen science, because access will be skewed by who has free time … and time is money, unfortunately.'

+

005

ECO
NOMIC
EMPO

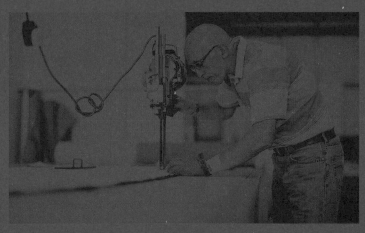
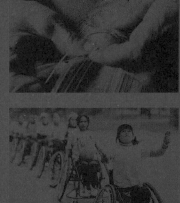

005
ECONOMIC EMPOWERMENT

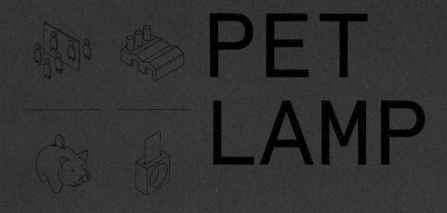

PET
LAMP

Using craftsmanship
and cultural skills to
address abundant
material waste

OPPOSITE:
+ 005EP/PL/02

+ 005EP/PL/01

+ 005EP/PL/03

+ 005EP/PL/04

++ The principal hypotheses out of which the PET Lamp project emerged are the possibility to approach a global problem (the waste from plastic PET bottles) with a local activity (the textile tradition).

+ 005EP/PL/05

Plastic PET bottles create huge pollution problems internationally, finding their way into waterways and oceans after heavy rain. The damage caused by the material's presence costs about $13 billion annually in losses for the tourism, shipping and fishing industries, disrupts marine ecosystems, and threatens food security for people dependent on subsistence fishing. The World Economic Forum predicts that, by 2050, the amount of plastics in the ocean will, pound for pound, outweigh fish. Plastic bottles are part of that waste, having a short lifespan compared to their production resources. In tropical locations, however, the collection and recycling of this material is fraught with systemic challenges. With this in mind the PET Lamp design team formed international alliances between local crafts organizations, textile/wicker workers and retailers (005EP/PL/01). The project, initiated in Colombia, was a design response to raise awareness of plastic-bottle disposal. The team commission unique outputs from regional craft practitioners (005EP/PL/03), delivering livelihoods to local makers through their traditional knowledge and practice (005EP/PL/04). The lamps use the bottle's body for structure, complemented by textile weaving techniques and engaging networks of practitioners in Colombia, Chile, Ethiopia, Japan, Australia and Thailand.

Items are completed with industry-/retailer-compliant fittings. Finished artefacts maintain unique provenance, through local skill sets, materials, colours, motifs and craft (005EP/PL/05). The intention is to establish a process of working with cultural undertones. Each

production location has different materials, treatments and aesthetics. For example, in Japan, bamboo is the material staple; in Ethiopia, grasses and palm leaves are woven; and in Chile (Chimbarongo), wicker is cultivated, farmed and woven, positively impacting the agricultural economies that surround local factories. PET Lamp's uniqueness leverages local communities' skills and cultures to make mutually fruitful, high-quality, saleable outcomes, promoting craft practice at scale. In interview, designer Alvaro Catalán de Ocón commented: 'We have always been conscious of how little we can impact on waste. We are proud of having sold over 15,000 lamps, which has helped keep the bottles out of waste streams. But it's really insignificant regarding the amount of bottles that are being produced and solving the problem for a short time, as sooner or later the lamps will break before the plastic is degraded ... [As designers] we have a strong power to communicate, which is part of our expertise. From the beginning we made a great effort to communicate the project [to reach] wider audiences, approaching it from a design, craft, ecological and social perspective. Involving these four contemporary issues is part of its success.'

From a local perspective, 'the project has helped the weavers since it started. In the PET Lamp brief they wanted the project to be economically self-sustained, making it real, and this will keep it going, the only way it can be helpful to weavers. PET Lamp collect lampshades once or twice a month and pay for them before they sell them. This way,

+ 005EP/PL/08

the weaver can plan their economy around the project, building a stock to respond quickly to their clients (005EP/PL/06). This also puts pressure on us to keep sales going and not wait for clients to call ... It's hard to sell crafts locally, as they are usually not appreciated and valued as they are when you put them out of their context. We give that extra value through design, spending time with the weavers in long workshops (005EP/PL/07), and then work hard in the details and electrical connections ... This way, we open their crafts to the design market and to clients they would have never dreamed of.'

Catalán de Ocón explained that weavers' collaborations run deeply through the project (005EP/PL/08). 'Imelda is one of our best Colombian weavers. She is an Eperara Siapidara weaver from the Cauca, displaced by the guerrilla war in Bogotá. She lived in a precarious situation four years ago, and now she takes her son to school, paying for a small house and employing weavers to build PET Lamps, building a small business around it. Segundo is a weaver from Chimbarongo, working in the wicker "capital" of Chile. Previously working as a bricklayer, his age was making it hard to maintain working outside in cold winters ... His real passion and expertise was in wicker weaving, but he could not make a living from it. Now he has retired and works from his house doing PET Lamps and other wicker products.'

Catalán de Ocón identified that projects need to be economically viable: 'If it's not, you are doing something wrong and should find where the problem comes from.' The organization has strong ethical values, considering it irresponsible to approach artisanal communities and create false expectations. His advice is to 'create a structure keeping the project running, both locally, to keep the production going, as well as globally, to sell and distribute them. The organization not only have their studio with independent responsibilities, but links with international satellite studios in countries who run the project building the workshops together, maintaining communication with artisans. They pride themselves on transparent communication with everyone: 'clients, weavers, shops, collaborators ... and that allows everyone to feel the project as part of themselves'. Finally, Catalán de Ocón stated: 'We don't gamble with weavers' payments, we create agreements according to other products they make, public organizations which assess us regarding payments ... and, according to this price, and the logistics around the country, we give a price to the lamp.' The project provides an exportable economy, reviving cultural craft practice, creating ecosystems around local skill sets and making importable manufacturing.

+ + The identity of each culture that has participated in the PET Lamp project is evident in each lamp.

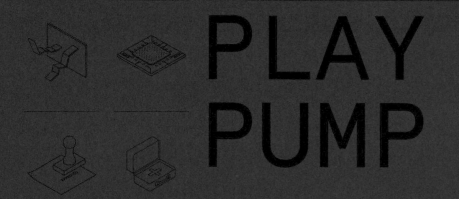

PLAY
PUMP

Making self–sustaining
products through
holistic design

+ 005EP/PP/01

+ 005EP/PP/02

+ 005EP/PP/03

South Africa is susceptible to drought. Cattle die, farmers cannot plant crops and rivers run dry. Worldwide, about 4,500 children die each day from unsafe water, with countless others suffering from poor health and diminishing education opportunities (005EP/PP/02). This is why supplying clean drinking water to rural South Africa is PlayPump's mission. Rural schools and local communities are reliant on generators and borehole pumps. PlayPumps look like a playground roundabout, but are connected to an underground water supply (005EP/PP/01). When motion is applied, the energy generated brings water up to the surface, where it is pumped into storage tanks. Anyone requiring water draws it from these tanks, either immediately or over time (005EP/PP/03). When the tank is full, excess water returns to the ground. In some communities, the water supply only gets turned on once or twice a week, or for a couple of hours a day, which is why the PlayPump is so important.

PlayPumps are especially well suited to schools. The founder (a farmer) thought 'he'd entertain the children while they used energy to pump water', and later donated the manufacturing rights to Roundabout Outdoor Pty Ltd. Children play to pump the water, and the equipment is located next to advertising boards to bring in revenue and support project sustainability and maintenance. PlayPump stated: 'There's water for washing hands after the children have been to the toilet, or before they eat meals, cook, etc. All schools in South Africa should provide a cooked meal for the children once a day, but obviously if they haven't got water they can't do that. People we want to provide water to are rural primary schools – we don't supply urban areas because there isn't a need.'

Maintenance is an important aspect. PlayPump originally expected the tank stand advertising to cover maintenance costs, but changed their tactics to generate fundraising instead. They carry out maintenance checks once every 18 months to 2 years. The biggest costs come from shipping manufactured spare parts from Johannesburg to various locations. The second challenge is finding suitable boreholes. PlayPump do not drill boreholes; they want to find existing boreholes with broken pumps, as they do not remove working equipment. Initially, they get community buy-in from schools, then test boreholes for their sustainability, and finally they check that the water quality is fit for human consumption, prior to equipment installation.

Commentators argue over whether a PlayPump is play or work. Some argue that children across Africa have to work anyway, especially when it comes to collecting water, and believe it is better to have children spin on a PlayPump than to undertake the grind of a hand pump.

PlayPump's cost is 125,000 South African Rand per unit, including finding the borehole, the community liaison work, all the equipment, manufacturing, transportation, deployment and installation by a trained team. With over 1,400 PlayPumps in circulation in South Africa, some require repair as they have been in use since the 1980s. Recurring feedback from schools is that they 'need help, because if there's no water the children get dehydrated: they get sent home early. They're not learning because they're dehydrated, they can't concentrate.' Once they've got a PlayPump, water is available, meaning children stay longer in school with improved concentration. Often in rural schools, if there is no water, it's the girls (from PlayPump's experience) who are sent out to collect water from rivers and dams that are often contaminated by animals defecating into the water while drinking, giving rise to waterborne diseases and diarrhoea, which are then transmitted to people who use the contaminated water.

PlayPump stated: 'If children know they're going to get a meal, they will attend school, because often it's their only meal of the day or it's their first meal of the day – a lot of them go to school hungry. They might get a meal in the evening, but their parents can't afford to feed them. A lot of them are orphans, so it's a child-headed household who probably hasn't got the money to feed their brothers and sisters. These schools are, especially the ones in very rural areas, desperately in need of clean water.' PlayPump's view on social design is to promote cultural empathy to make sure organizations have community buy-in: 'People mustn't go rushing in and think that they can do it all. They should realize that they might be taking a job away from somebody' – a wise lesson.

+ 005EP/M/01

Raising quality of
life through local
manufacture, trade
and repair

MOTIVATION

+ + Good design is all about improving people's quality of life. For me, thoughtful design and engineering have enabled me to travel, go to work and be independent.

+ 005EP/M/02

Motivation was conceived through a design competition and the vision of supporters from the Royal College of Art, and is now approaching its third decade. The team was formed by two students, one a wheelchair user, informed by travel experiences and encouraged by the RCA rector. Motivation design and provide low-cost wheelchairs within appropriate and sustainable restrictions. Initially, the organization was global – establishing small, local workshops and refurbishing local factories with partner organizations throughout Asia, Africa, Central America and Eastern Europe. They initially set up 22 workshops in 18 different countries, so in 10 years they have made around 18,000 wheelchairs (005EP/M/02).

Motivation established the project so wheelchair users could revisit either that partner group (workshop) or local/international organization and have their chair repaired. The process caters for people whose circumstances change, meaning that they require a chair replacement or to be reassessed. It is not solely a product production company; it carefully considers its surrounding service. The organization believes in the vision of creating embedded knowledge and a 'social side' of knowledge that remains in the community. Their cornerstone was creating a flexible product that could be fitted on site for size flexibility, was suitable for the environment the user was living in, and was repairable with replacement parts locally. Their first major insight was not just the design but how they created training packages for construction, fit and local repair. The organization then went through strategic change. Their mantra

was originally 'make local', until they decided that, actually, they could probably flat-pack the wheelchairs from a central manufacturing location to maintain a good standard of quality and a low price, reaching more people.

Founded as a charity, Motivation added a social enterprise, wholly owned by the charity, in 2009, enabling sales of products to other humanitarian organizations. Any profits that the enterprise generates are returned to the business, which is the definition of social enterprise: bringing in an income, creating surpluses, but with a social-benefit bottom line. Motivation are delivering commissions to charity, providing mobility through their social enterprise. After design, testing and deployment in various countries, they saw emerging patterns. They realized that making adjustable units and fitting the wheelchair to the user was critical, transforming their thinking. Their primary work is not solely wheelchair manufacture but also providing training and establishing a service that users can visit, and then be assessed, prescribed, fitted, and followed by a product. Those three elements – products, service and training – work together for positive outputs. The International Paralympic Committee (IPC), International Tennis Federation (ITF) and International Wheelchair Basketball Federation (IWBF) requested Motivation to design a low-cost, entry-level sports wheelchair, and organizations and users have since adopted the chair worldwide (005EP/M/03).

Motivation has also been engaged on a policy level, informing good codes of practice. As a

OVERLEAF:
+ 005EP/M/03

OPPOSITE:
+ 005EP/M/04

+ FUTUREKIND
+ 005 ECONOMIC EMPOWERMENT

+ MOTIVATION

+ 177

+ 005EP/M/05

result of the 2006 Consensus conference, the World Health Organization (WHO) published 'Guidelines on the Provision of Manual Wheelchairs in Less Resourced Settings'. This was a turning point in the sector of wheelchair provision. By 2010, this was the most downloaded set of guidelines from the WHO website. These guidelines have been translated into all UN languages, and remain the most important document in the international wheelchair sector. This unification of processes has now become an industry requirement, changing the construction of these life-changing products. However, a Motivation wheelchair stands for so much more than simply a vehicle to transport someone from A to B. They believe it has the power to both empower and instil confidence to help disabled people in developing countries to lead active, fulfilled and happy lives.

Motivation's wheelchairs look and work better through careful design (005EP/M/04). Their factories work with the rationale of informed production, because they do not believe in sending a box to merely sit on a shelf and turn to dust because no one needs its contents (005EP/M/05). They are currently exploring new routes to distribution through digital manufacture. The main risk in distributing manufacture digitally – or through conventional

channels – is achieving 'repeatable quality'. They set the WHO standards for wheelchair design. The founder stated that 'it has been easier to gain financial support to pay for finished products, but more difficult to encourage investment in design and development.' The social side of the project is that they do not just sell wheelchairs; they provide training to make sure that people are able to assess and prescribe a chair properly, and adjust it. If they were just a business, they would simply sell them. Motivation expressed their belief that social design is something that really, truly meets the needs of the contextual society, addressing the beneficiaries who can afford it in an appropriate, sustainable manner. Finally, the project has now yielded a range of sports wheelchairs that have helped foster and develop grassroots sport in over 60 countries worldwide.

Motivation really understand the term 'appropriate', demonstrated in their fit-for-purpose construction and delivery models. They also understand what it takes to truly make something affordable. It is interesting to note that Motivation has gone from local production to off-shoring production, and are now returning to a more bespoke approach to the production/fitting of wheelchairs and seating using digital technologies that didn't exist when they were founded.

+ + Our mission statement is to enhance the quality of life for people with mobility disabilities. The key words in that are 'quality of life'.

HIUT
DENIM

Job creation using
local skills, achieved
through compelling
storytelling

+ 005EP/HD/01

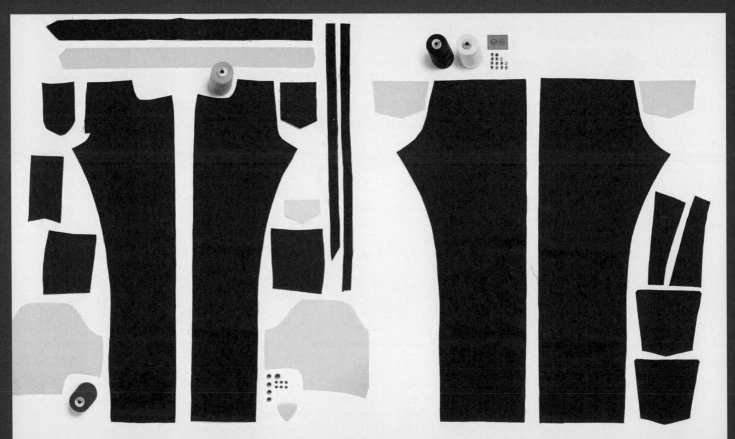

+ 005EP/HD/02

+ 005EP/HD/03

In November 2002, Dewhirst womenswear told their 400-strong workforce that their biggest customer, M&S, were moving manufacturing to Morocco. Overnight, one in ten of Cardigan's 4,000 people were unemployed. The Welsh town was home to Britain's largest jeans factory, making an average of 35,000 pairs of jeans a week for four decades. Nine years later, entrepreneur David Hieatt reinstated the town's denim legacy, launching Hiut Denim. Hiut claims to be the only British brand making its own jeans in its own factory. Its core mission is 'Do one thing well'. Hiut's unique selling point is that the jeans use raw denim. Hiut's material choice and manufacturing considerations reduce the environmental impact, compared to alternative brands. Hiuts cost around £130 to £230 (005EP/HD/03), and are designed to last a lifetime: quality over quantity. Hiut buyers find each pair uniquely numbered, and when registered, owners can see their jeans being crafted by Jean, Amanda or Elin. The Hieatts established the 'Do Lectures', a biannual event of socially engaged talks and workshops for leading thinkers (like TED, but in rural Wales).

The Hieatts are great storytellers; they not only create high-quality artefacts, but they are also fantastic at communicating their story. Their firm started with an Instagram account, gaining support from acclaimed bands and celebrities. In interview, Hieatt stated that their core mission was 'to get 400 people their jobs back, plain and simple'. Craftsmanship and making are core to their outlook: ['We] have 75 different processes to making our jeans and we only have to be world-class at 75 of them. It is a handcrafted product that we make, and what I say to everybody in the factory is, it is my ambition for us is to make the best jeans we can, not the most jeans we can. We make a product that we want to literally sign because we are proud of it. Just like a carpenter would sign a piece of work they were incredibly proud of, or an artist would sign something.' When asked about their biggest impact, Hieatt responded: 'The town will regain its confidence; the economic impact of 400 people being employed will be huge. Also a greater thing is we won't have lost the skills of making; we are fighting each day for the right to make. It is about retaining skills in a town; if you spent 40 years learning something, then it

is important that we pass those skills on. We live in a world where people design and they get someone else to make. If you want to be really incredible at something you have got to be able to design, prototype and make.'

Industrial challenges still remain: 'Starting a factory is hard; that is why most people don't do it ... In that time between the factory closing and us thinking about starting Hiut, the internet happened, [and] there was a resurgence in craft and respect for the maker. If you look at coffee and craft beer, it is a special time because, for the small maker, there is more interest in quality and the internet allows you to sell to that customer. If we did this five or ten years ago it would have been impossible because the timing would have been wrong and the internet wouldn't have been ready. Actually, people wouldn't have the interest in high quality, buying something once and making it last like they do now ... [Important lessons are] the importance of starting and not just talking about what you are going to do. Quality and the importance of design is paramount. People should put their emphasis on building a team and community, building a brand that people not just buy from but feel something for is critical ... the only thing that matters is everything.'

Hieatt's view on spreading the message through social technologies is compelling. 'We are completely blessed by the technology that we have. Our stories travel further, faster and freer than ever before. When I stand on stage and tell people we are going to get 400 people their jobs back, nobody is laughing anymore. It is no longer impossible. If we can make one of the finest pairs of jeans on the planet ... we can then go and tell the world about them with extraordinary tools – Instagram, Twitter, Medium, Facebook – all these incredible tools [give us] the ability to try and pull off something that would have been impossible ten years ago. These social tools allow us a dialogue and a communication with our customer that is almost unrivalled on Planet Earth.' While this company has simple, clear and brand-oriented objectives, the community they work within drives them. Often people designing artefacts think about the touch, the feel, the emotion, the brand ... but designing to provide employment is a pretty good global lesson.

+ 005EP/S/01

Solving identity crisis
through cultural
understanding

SIMPRINTS

+ 005EP/S/02

The World Bank says that more than 1.5 billion people (one in five) internationally do not officially exist, lacking formal identification. Simprints are a non-profit tech company transforming identification, through biometric technology that is 228% more accurate than that currently used. Their goal is to eliminate these inaccuracies to track and deliver social impact. Their open-source software and biometric hardware builds on mobile tools used by NGOs and governments fighting poverty internationally (005EP/S/01). Alexandra Grigore, Simprints' co-founder, and Nathaniel Giraitis, strategy director of Smart Design, shared their experiences.

'[Simprints' mission] is building, deploying and sustaining the world's most accessible identification tools, ending poverty and preventable suffering (005EP/S/02). We are building systems to enable people without formal ID to access services in healthcare, education, finance, etc. Imagine life without ID, making it near impossible to access services, especially in developing countries, i.e. sub-Saharan Africa or South Asia ... [We recognized that medics] were unable to identify people: you enrol patients, provide treatment and five months later, that patient returns. It is impossible to find records

because patients don't know their date of birth or have unique identifiers.' Giraitis stated that 'my focus was defining design research methodologies to uncover insights, ensuring our designs were appropriately user-centred. There are feedback loops in the private world – i.e. selling – something sells poorly, it's going poorly. In the non-profit world, it's a well-deserving idea, or the ideal tech, but they don't create user-centred impact.'

During the Simprints collaboration, 'Smart Design wasn't providing physical designs, but teaching mechanisms to deploy design and research methods. We're working with an NGO called "BRAC", the largest development NGO in the world, serving 90 million people in Bangladesh. One project within maternal healthcare equipped community health workers with identification tools, ensuring that pregnant mothers get antenatal care visits. Community health workers trekked house to house within their region to ensure treatments to pregnant mothers ... [The] first time we asked people to use the scanners, they placed their fingers incorrectly. The boxed technology wasn't enough, requiring an additional layer of user experience enabling impact in daily life ... [We] thought it's easy to keep your finger straight, but for people with arthritis or those excessively

+ + The boxed technology wasn't enough to solve the problem, requiring an additional layer of user experience to take a solution and make an impact on daily life.

OVERLEAF:
+ 005EP/S/03

+ 184

+ FUTUREKIND
+ 005 ECONOMIC EMPOWERMENT

+ SIMPRINTS

OPPOSITE:
+ 005EP/S/05

+ + Simprints' mission builds, deploys and sustains the world's most accessible identification tools, ending poverty and preventable suffering.

+ 005EP/S/04

working in fields, they can't straighten their fingers. In Bangladesh we worked with community health workers designing solutions that we're now using in other contexts (005EP/S/04). We interviewed and shadowed community health workers, contextually understanding their lives, and will be scaling that project to reach 4.8 million pregnant mothers.'

Smart Design highlighted the 'importance of empowering teams with methodologies, to understand cultural meanings of symbols: thumbs up, thumbs down, green, red? As we imparted user-centred knowledge to Simprints, they worked with the NGOs in Bangladesh, passing knowledge by proxy [and] creating community ambassadors. When the Simprints team flew back to Cambridge, connections remained in Bangladesh to remotely get feedback to improve designs, for and with end recipients. Having local ambassadors for continual feedback and improvement of the solution is something they're building into future contracts with NGOs internationally.'

Simprints categorically stated: 'If you want to design any technology with a social purpose, get to know your users. A lot of groups want to develop a technology for developing countries without going there. You need to go, to build champions, because you won't get real-time feedback ... [You] have to go there, and you won't be able to fly there more than once every few months. You can't spend more than a few weeks, at most, with your users. It's very critical to train user champions. Making sure that you have the right training in place

and the right knowledge transfer protocols or methods to train people in the field to pass on appropriate feedback (005EP/S/05). Before the feedback starts, going there and making sure that you include the users in a lot of the co-creation exercises. Everything is contextual; you won't speak the same language as your users. It's critical to train translators, and not just hire them to translate. We identified that translators weren't capturing people's subtle communications, leading to translator training prior to user feedback in the field.'

Finally, '[adapting] design methodologies for social development contexts is critical. We tried intuition tests, shadowing, card sorting and co-creation so users make personal designs. [You need to be] flexible and [admit that] not all methods work in contexts. You get more information by having people choosing visually with prototypes rather than asking "What do you think about this?" We spent days in the field without useful information because translators asked excessive leading questions, and not encouraging users to be honest with feedback ... [There] needs to be continued engagement. You need to build tools and mechanisms for feedback and anticipate a tail to that impact story; it's not just for the end beneficiaries, but it's by the end beneficiaries.'

AZUKO

Designing within
communities,
empowering
through design

+ 005EP/AK/01

+ 005EP/AK/02

AzuKo is the name of this non-profit architectural practice, and translates as 'all of humanity'. Their mission is to improve lives in areas with limited assets through community-driven, research-based design initiatives, while remaining sensitive to local contexts. They aim to design with disadvantaged communities, empowering them to create the world they dream of. The idea is not to build or design for them, but to facilitate communities' own design process. AzuKo believes in trans-disciplinary design, incorporating economists, political figures, local artists and the end user from the start (005EP/AK/02). They pride themselves on their human-centred design processes and incorporate values of trust, respect and understanding as fundamental to their holistic design process. Their approach is research-driven, and they believe there are no shortcuts to sustainable development.

AzuKo focuses on gathering the right data, understanding that there are no universal answers: that progress can be made through an accumulation of small steps based on careful analysis of unique situations. The team has consulted for the World Bank on projects to undertake a human-centred analysis of their cyclone shelter programme (005EP/AK/03). AzuKo is 'supporting Jogen Babu Maath slum

[to] improve the living conditions, with the design of community sanitation and drainage'. The project seeks to empower the people of Jogen Babu Maath in Bangladesh to make their own changes and form organizations in an effort to rise out of poverty, with the intention of avoiding an unsustainable dependence on aid. Here, Jo Ashbridge, founder of AzuKo, shares her insights.

'[AzuKo is a registered charity] pushing the idea of community-led design, to build capacity, to support communities in leading their own projects … [Our work in] Jogen Babu Maath is a sanitation facility. The community designed, managed and built it, [and] we hope that they will be able to fix it themselves. They will be able to go to markets and haggle for parts, because they know what the right parts are. They understand the mechanics but also the financing. We hope they can operate, maintain and manage the building for the next 20 years plus … [and] continue to imagine what the future could be for this urban informal settlement.' AzuKo facilitated a democratic election, establishing a committee as a community voice in the design process. They 'worked with communities throughout the project, from the need assessments, understanding needs and prioritizing them. Working on the financial

+ + AzuKo's mission is to improve lives in areas with limited assets through community-driven, research-based design initiatives that are sensitive to local contexts.

OVERLEAF:
+ 005EP/AK/03

Sanitation facility Plan
Jogen Babu Maath

22 November 2016

OPPOSITE:
+ 005EP/AK/04

+ FUTUREKIND
+ 005 ECONOMIC EMPOWERMENT

+ AZUKO

+ 191

+ 005EP/AK/05

model, budgeting, documentation, gathering metrics and understanding the impact of this project. Designing the solutions, and in this case, the first pilot is going to be one of a series.'

To understand their impact, they 'have been undertaking an interview process with all the committee members over the last month, to understand the soft and hard skills that they believe they have improved over the last two years, working with us on this specific project. The entire committee have seen improvements in different areas. From soft skills, like working with others, and showing empathy to another member of your community and listening to their perspective, [to] harder skills, like understanding financial systems and creating budgets. It's not just an impact that the building exists and people are using it. They have access to clean water, sanitation and hygiene, while building different skills.'

AzuKo's insights highlight the importance of communities – '[they want more] design professionals, taking on social impact design, or considering it as a career. The more people, the more competitive and the better the sector will be. That said, when you come out of design school, you have skills, tools, the methods to create. You don't necessarily have development, or economics or politics skills. Graduates shouldn't immediately lead these development projects, whether they are local, national or international. Maybe

they embed themselves within existing organizations, which have been working in local contexts, learning and building from there.'

One key point is that 'good intentions are great, but you can also create harm, especially when you are working with vulnerable communities or in a fragile context (005EP/ AK/04). Understanding that you need to know more before you start leading such projects is key ... [Whenever] we embark on a project, it is really important to understand who the local [partners] are. Whether they are individuals in a community, or whether they are a key local partner. Working with them to design and implement the project. We couldn't do it without our local partners, and nor should we. They are the people that understand the context, and the holistic response to interventions. Local partners are absolutely key (005EP/AK/05). It's not always easy.' In their projects, they try to 'design ourselves out of business. To be able to support communities, so that when we leave, they have the skills, capacity and confidence to continue upgrading and improving their living conditions. Yes, we are trying to put ourselves out of business. That's the goal.'

+ + AzuKo focuses on gathering the right data, understanding that there are no universal answers and that progress can be made through an accumulation of small steps based on careful analysis of unique situations.

+ 005EP/OD/01

Linking designers,
makers and customers
to deliver furniture

OPENDESK

+ 005EP/OD/02

Opendesk is an international network that links designers, customers and local makers to fabricate and deliver furniture (005EP/OD/01). They believe that making things locally and on-demand - using distributed manufacturing - is a more resource-efficient way to produce, as it eliminates shipping, warehousing and waste. The model supports local fabricators during idle CNC machine time, and leads to distributed employment through manufacture (005EP/OD/02).

In an interview, co-founder Joni Steiner began by revealing the narrative behind the project. 'Nick [Ierodiaconou] and I started Opendesk as architects particularly interested in the process of making - as being close to making enables inputs and feedback.' He says the organization exemplifies designer and educator Bruce Mau's belief in 'being more interested in the design of the world than the world of design'. 'Opendesk started by experimenting with a CNC machine, and making blueprints for products available for download. The process enables anyone to buy plywood, CNC-cut the parts in a local

FabLab, then finish and assemble themselves … A tech company in London challenged us to design their office with a small budget in a short time frame, and through this we learned about digital fabrication. We found latent capacity in digital-fabrication workshops – like the one run by Ian Jinks, the first fabricator we worked with. This company also had an office in New York, and requested the same furniture to be shipped there. In the same way that you might email a PDF to print 10,000 copies of a book in New York, we realized that we could email and "print" furniture locally. In this way, Opendesk builds on John Maynard Keynes's dictum that "it's easier to ship recipes than cakes and biscuits" – you're not moving goods, you're moving information, with the benefits of local production. If you're in New York, you have a New York maker, in Paris a Parisian maker, and so on, using the scale of cities.'

Opendesk found 'existing CNC businesses with machining capacity, in particular Renatus, which makes church organs in Devon. They contacted us, meeting the requirements of an "Opendesk

+ + The most important thing is ensuring that people – your core market, core customers, core makers and designers – are all benefiting. Then grow that core, rather than trying to spread yourself too thinly.

+ 005EP/OD/03

+ 005EP/OD/04

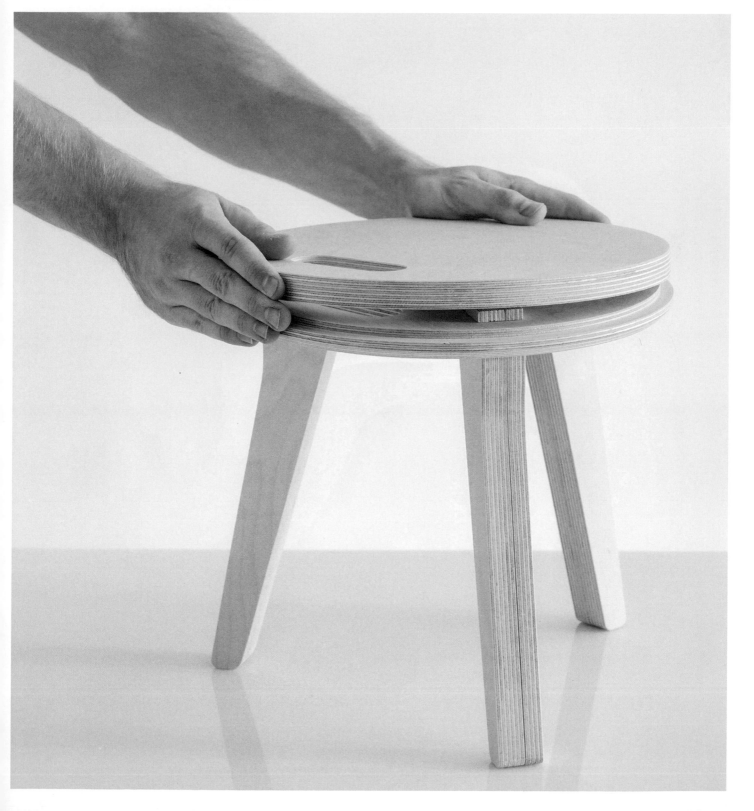

+ + We found there were CNC businesses with spare machining capacity.

+ 005EP/OD/05

+ 005EP/OD/06

+ 005EP/OD/07

+ 005EP/OD/08

+ + If you approach things in a more open way, you do see benefits for all. Denis Fuzii went from never meeting us to having his chair all over the Olympic Park. Fuzii even said his current work is built off that moment of sharing.

+ 005EP/OD/09

maker". They are exceptional craftspeople, and the church organ market fluctuates financially. It takes 18 months to make a church organ, with CNC idle time, so we joined up. Their skills, latent capacity and machine downtime can be optimized to produce something outside their core business while providing business sustenance ... [We thought] this fits into our mission of distributing the making of things, and we don't want subcontractors (005EP/OD/05). We want amazing craftspeople when they have time, we're fitting around them, we're working for them, not them for us.'

'[Opendesk's core] mission is to empower a network of independent designer makers to create beautiful furniture locally (005EP/OD/08). It's about building a global equitable and distributed supply chain; by starting with how we design and make things, we can build a healthier future. A lot of our problems are based around our consumption and don't consider the ecosystem around that consumption. We're not interested in just selling desks. Our mission is to change how desks are made and sold for the better – and then move on to other products. We have an openly shared charter outlining how we want to work, making our mission and values transparent to all.'

Opendesk see themselves as '[a] distribution channel for emerging designers, without an audience. It's difficult for young designers to break into companies. One of our first designers, Denis Fuzii, a Brazilian in São Paulo, designed the Valoví chair. He said, "I'm happy for you to publish it on the platform", trusting us [and]

establishing when you share things everyone wins. We always clearly articulate how users want to license their design ... [Fuzii] chose a Creative Commons licence, allowing people to make his chair for themselves; if made commercially, he gets a financial percentage. We were doing a project for the former Olympic Park, converting the ex-broadcasting centre into innovation office spaces. They were looking for chairs, with a quick local turnaround. Fuzii went from never meeting us, to having his chair all over the Olympic Park. Fuzii even said his current work is built off that moment of sharing. If you approach things in a more open way, you do see benefits for all.'

Opendesk's experience and insight is from 'working with different designers with openness and curiosity (005EP/OD/06). It's not for everybody, and I think being open-minded and generous has benefited us. Being open and agnostic is quite powerful, because you listen to everyone's position. Your actions speak louder than words. We've realized there are times you have to be outward looking and then maintain focus; as a start-up we've gone through cycles of that. The most important thing is ensuring that people – your core market, core customers, core makers and designers – are all benefiting. Then grow that core, rather than trying to spread yourself too thinly.'

+

∅∅

006
ACCESS TO KNOWLEDGE

6 ACCESS TO KNOWLEDGE

WONDER
SPHERE

Designing for wellbeing
in a heavily restricted
environment

+ 006ATK/W/02

Hospitalized children and adolescents, including those with chronic illnesses, experience pain, fear, boredom and isolation from the natural world – but children with compromised immune systems can't be around plants and natural objects. To counter this, Katie Stoudemire brings the outdoors inside, making nature accessible. The WonderSphere is a sealed, mobile chamber that empowers paediatric patients through multi-sensory learning experiences, promoting joy and wellbeing. Built-in gloves enable hospitalized children to plant, dig, water and touch nature without danger of infection. The Wonder Connection programme increases patients' science knowledge and inspires them for the future; it is supported by grants and donations. The natural science activities are patient-centred, focusing on empowering patients and giving them opportunities to make choices and be creative. Wonder Connection's mission is based on research demonstrating better health outcomes for hospital patients who experience positive emotions and/or nature-based activities, making it easier for them to heal (006ATK/W/01).

The technical challenge was to create a gas-tight seal in order to protect users from natural materials harbouring bacteria, viruses and fungi – while enabling children to interact with materials inside the WonderSphere, and teachers to change the contents. After interaction with WonderSphere patients have been shown to feel happier, proud, distracted from pain and actively engaged with something external to their healthcare state. Wonder Connection founder Katie Stoudemire hired BresslerGroup to design and build the WonderSphere.

'[Nature] can be inspiring,' notes Stoudemire, 'healing and full of hope. Also, it's a great way to engage people, but these kids were separated from it so ... Instead of putting a kid inside a bubble, we'll put the plant inside the bubble and let the kids interact with it ... [The] Wonder Connection programme with the WonderSphere aspires to make kids happy, helping them engage and experience other positive emotions ... to date all participants have agreed ... [There are] so many stories; one that springs to mind is a young child going through chemotherapy

who could not have flowers in her room, but was able to do a flower arrangement inside the WonderSphere. She worked with her mum to create a beautiful arrangement (006ATK/W/02). Then she decided she wanted to give the flower arrangement to another child across the hall, making a connection. At one point she stated, "Hey, this is better than an iPad." In today's world, that's a huge compliment ... [I am] not a designer; in terms of how I would define this project, it's like we're using design to address this problem that these kids have and this disconnection that they have, and to use design to help make that connection – both a physical connection to nature, wonder and joy.'

'We wanted to use design to solve the problem of kids not being able to touch nature, because it could make them sick. We assembled a team with Wonder Connection, BresslerGroup and the hospital, and developed a relationship with the epidemiology department (infection control). They ensure that whatever you're doing in the hospital is safe for the patients. Particularly in this case, if we're bringing items to multiple patients' rooms. Infection control responded, "We believe you when you say that you want this to be safe. We're going to help you make sure it's safe." They also stated, "Usually, people come to us after they've already designed something and they're like, Here, what do you think?" I went to them before we started: "I didn't know what parameters we would need to test it, but maybe you can help me." That was the biggest piece, pulling in partners, that ultimately decides "Is this safe or not?" ... [Then another] interesting piece has been, when originally designed, we thought that we would be using it primarily for planting stuff, but actually the programming has evolved. I should have thought more about that before I started, although I doubt it would have changed the design. At this point now, taking time to really think about how we use it for programming, beyond just the simple "we put stuff in it and it's safe", has been just something that's been hard to make time for. The follow-through on things is really important, [and we needed to ask] "How are we really using it?" The key lessons are establishing partners early even before designing has been commissioned, identify holistic barriers to entry and think more about content and engagement post design delivery.'

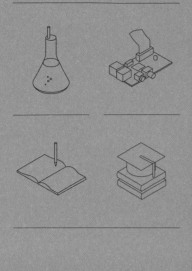

OPPOSITE:
+ 006ATK/ELP/02

Designing for
communication
and protection

ELEPHANT LISTENING PROJECT

+ + We've got a long way to go still, to convince people to stop buying ivory, and to care about forest elephants. Outreach is an important part of the work, although it's difficult to monitor our impact.

+ 006ATK/ELP/03

Elephants are under siege throughout Africa, with ivory demands increasing and poaching now affecting forest elephants. Forests in the Central African Republic and the Congo are being transformed by logging roads, opening up previously remote regions to poachers (006ATK/ELP/03). The Elephant Listening Project (ELP) was founded by Katy Payne in 1999. A few years earlier, she had discovered that the Asian elephants she was studying in Portland Zoo were using frequencies to communicate that were inaudible to human ears. ELP now uses autonomous recording units (ARUs) to continuously record elephant vocalizations in forested areas. The ARUs are elevated in trees, protecting them from elephant damage, so they can constantly record elephant vocalizations, gunshots and the sounds of other species.

The main idea behind eavesdropping on elephants is to provide data on elephant numbers in different areas and at different times, which is essential for planning conservation strategies. ELP is also studying how the vocalizations relate to behaviours. This information could make the long-term recordings even more useful. After the recordings have been collected, the sound data are analysed using a sound visualization

program. With many thousands of hours to examine, this is a challenge. The elephant rumbles can be difficult to identify because there are many other sounds that 'look' and sound similar to a distant rumble.

Researcher Liz Rowland shared the team's insights: '[The ELP's mission is to] understand forest elephants' behaviour and movements by using acoustics, primarily with the goal of conserving forest elephants and their habitats.' To date one of their biggest impacts has been in detecting gunshots: 'People are excited about gunshot detection, because that's the prime reason for the elephants' demise. At the moment, we can provide information on where and when gunshots were recorded over the duration of the recording (usually 3 months), so the data aren't real-time. Nevertheless, it has been useful because we can show where the poaching was worst, and whether there were any temporal patterns, such as in time of day, day of the week, or seasonal patterns. We hope that eventually we will have a real-time system. When a gunshot was recorded, it would automatically be detected and an alert would be sent by satellite to a cell phone or laptop so that the anti-poaching team would immediately know where and when a gun had been fired. A team of anti-poaching guards (006ATK/ELP/04) would

+ + The Elephant Listening Project continuously record elephant vocalizations in forested areas. The recording units are in trees, protecting them from elephant damage, and constantly recording vocalizations, gunshots and the sounds of other species.

+ 006ATK/ELP/04

be deployed to find poachers … [At the moment] we're a way from this, because the technology is so difficult to resolve in the Congo, with no cell phone reception, and the dense rainforest prevents satellite reception. Furthermore, any data transmission requires a lot of power, and at the moment we're limited to battery power. The humidity also presents an engineering challenge. So, in theory, it's all possible, but it's just very, very difficult in the rainforest.'

'[In the] bioacoustics research programme, [we have] been using underwater recorders that capture whale calls in Massachusetts Bay. If detectors pick up a suspected right whale call, it sends that sound clip via satellite to a website so that we check whether it really is such a call. If it is, we can contact shipping in the area and ask it to slow down.'

'The main issue was, "Can acoustics be a more useful method to monitor elephant numbers than current methods?" We have shown that it is possible on a small scale, and now we are scaling up. If we are successful in that, then that will be another huge step, because we'll get, finally, more accurate information about where these elephants are at the landscape level.' In Rowlands' opinion, you have to always be striving for the next step in terms

of technological advances, because these will only be made if there is a need for them. There are many different problems; funding is one of the biggest, especially because many people don't see the immediate human benefit. To many people, saving elephants is just esoteric. As with any research, we spend a lot of time searching for funds. Finally, part of our goal, our mission, is to educate people, because unless people care about elephants worldwide, then there's no hope. I think that's always the basic principle of conservation really; to engage your audience in the first place so that they care enough to support the cause … [One] study showed that more illegal ivory is sold in America than in China. We've got a long way to go still, to convince people to stop buying ivory, and to care about forest elephants. Outreach is definitely an important part of the work, even though it's sometimes difficult to assess our impact on the general public.'

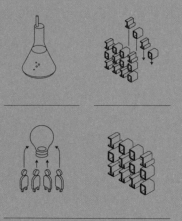

+ 006ATK/SC/01

Open platforms
for citizens to empower
themselves through
data capture

SMART
CITIZEN

+ 006ATK/SC/02

+ 006ATK/SC/03

+ 006ATK/SC/04

Since 2012, Smart Citizen has developed tools to support participatory sensing (006ATK/SC/01). This is an instrument ecosystem that gives people a more active role in 'the production of their city'. They believe that empowering communities to collect data from local environments can contribute to an interactive, worldwide environmental database through an open-source platform comprising three technological layers: hardware device, website/online API, and a mobile app. Smart Citizen is the world's largest independent environmental sensing network, connecting data, people and knowledge. The platform's objective is to serve as a node for building productive and open indicators and distributed tools, and the collective construction of the city for its own inhabitants. In interview, founder Tomas Diez explained: 'The first version focused on the urban environment and the pollution of air and noise, [and] also the temperature and humidity to basically allow people to capture this data in a very high-resolution, cost-effective way.' The kit is an average size of a pack of cards (006ATK/SC/03), and holds an 'Ambient Board' – a piece of hardware with two printed circuit boards, an interchangeable daughterboard, or 'shield', and an Arduino-compatible data-processing board. The kits measure carbon monoxide, nitrogen oxide, temperature, humidity, light and sound. Once set up, the kit wirelessly streams data to the Smart Citizen network (006ATK/SC/04).

The kit's low power consumption enables remote placement outdoors. The modular design (006ATK/SC/02) allows for users' additions such as WiFi antennas, permanent power supplies and solar panels. The core mission of Smart Citizen is to make technology accessible for everyone to have an active role in their city. In this case, it is capturing and sharing data to understand pollution causes in the city. As Diaz elaborated: 'The organization seeks to make technology accessible for people to use in a more productive way. They are now in a different digital divide, in which a lot of people have access to technology. Generalizing [on data contributions] is not contributing, it is really destructive, it is not helping people to be productive somehow. It is the other way around, it is creating dependencies of technology and consumption.' The Smart

Citizen team not only focus on sensors, but also the infrastructure to establish and maintain them ... they want people as part of the infrastructure. The data is sent to an open-source platform, and is accessible online. Smart Citizen also offer a family of APIs for people to develop beyond that data, empowering them to repurpose and reuse the data.

Diaz highlighted the original thinking: 'When we started to talk about Smart Citizen, everybody was just talking about smart cities. Our point was: if you want smart cities, we need to have smart citizens; the two require connecting. If you look at the transition of the language and also in the discourse around smart cities, it is now changing the human side of the city and not the technology side.' Their discourse and collaborators are influential, including government bodies and corporations with leading technology pioneers. Their core message is 'accessible knowledge through open-source platforms available for anyone, not only to use it, but also to modify it. [We face] challenges to ensure economic sustainability. It could be data, which creates funding streams, selling the hardware or consultancy. But we want to build that range of products and services our team can offer, to economically sustain ourselves.'

'We need to encourage responsible design, in relation [to] the impact on the environment of the products we bring to life. We should not only encourage participation but also stimulate similar practices in the development, conception, prototyping and distribution of products ... [We have a] need to encourage, aligning manufacturing and local skill, as we can see in the US, or even in the UK, but to also sustain the local production with a highly connected world. That is going to help reduce the environmental impact ... while creating business opportunities, impacting society as a whole.' The repeatable lessons create an empowered community, letting them take ownership ... but taking years to build. They had buy-in at the perfect governmental and local level, establishing an informed conversation and inviting the public to become participants. Finally, they empowered local champions and advocates to not only publicise activities, but to co-create with diverse audiences, moving non-users into empowered positions.

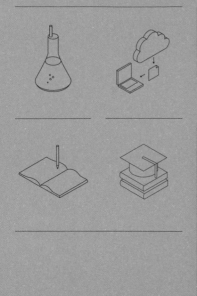

+ 006ATK/FS/01

Redesigning equipment
for education and
healthcare

FOLDSCOPE

+ 006ATK/FS/02

+ 006ATK/FS/03

Microscopes are a ubiquitous tool in science laboratories, but are expensive to maintain. Foldscope is a microscope made out of paper, assembled using origami, costing less than $1 to manufacture. It has five parts: a ball lens, a button battery, an LED, a switch and copper tape all pressed or bonded onto the paper. Despite the simplistic construction, Foldscope is capable of real science. With perforations marking the scope's components, and colour-coded elements for easy assembly, it offers a magnification of up to 2,100 times, with lower-spec versions offering 400 times (006ATK/FS/01). Founder Mr Prakash said 'you can throw it into water, stand on it, jump on it or throw it from a five-storey building'. They aim to manufacture 1 billion microscopes annually, getting children scientifically engaged and providing better diagnostic capabilities for diseases like E. coli and malaria. Foldscope have distributed 50,000 items to 135 countries, asking participants to share their findings online, such as identifying agricultural pests in India, cataloguing soil biodiversity in the Amazon, detecting fake currency, exposing water sample bacteria, and so on. Max Coyle, director of Foldscope's community engagement, offered insights.

'[Foldscope was] inspired by visiting India, Kenya and Tanzania. We repeatedly saw communities with broken or equipment access issues ... [Our core mission is] making science education experiential, putting the power of making discoveries into audiences beyond professional scientists, external to Western and wealthy countries ... [Malaria kills] hundreds of thousands of people every year; millions are at risk, and one challenge for malaria is obtaining accurate diagnoses. It's treatable if diagnosed correctly, but accurate identification is costly, and sometimes impossible. The gold standard for malaria diagnosis is a microscopic classification. If you get a blood smear on a microscope you can identify the parasite by seeing it, enabling diagnosis. The main infrastructural question is "If microscopy is required for malaria diagnosis, how do we make it as cheaply as possible?" The other converging thread was the idea of adding "experience" to science education, that is taught through rote. Especially in places lacking resources, we have an idea

that information is cheap, but experience is expensive ... [For example in a visited school we] had plenty of books, to develop cell theory understanding, but the experience of exploring a biological sample, like a leaf or pond water, was totally novel (006ATK/FS/03). They were absolutely thrilled to look under the Foldscope witnessing individual cells and the evidence for theories they were being taught.'

'[Foldscope] has two main themes, health and education, that are interrelated. Partnering groups are interested in clean water education, and enabling international communities to see parasites in their drinking water makes a difference, because people realize that, by exploring the world around me, I [can] discover things that make a tangible difference to my health and that of my community.' Foldscope's lessons include cost accessibility, mentorship, community building, training and project sustainability ... [However] you can't just dump 1,000 Foldscopes in schools and think science education is going to be transformed. The work is done by mentorship and interactions with those students ... [The Foldscope is an] opportunity for that interaction to happen, it connects people, [providing] a common tool that's very accessible, cheap and easy to use. So it's a microscope, but it's also a point of social connection.' Their advice is that 'fostering engagement is hugely important. We've had the most success in places where the engagement and follow-through have been thorough. Our locations of least success have been programmes where someone goes on a trip taking 200 Foldscopes with them. They leave them in a community where they don't exchange the knowledge, training and inspiration ... [This idea of] sustainable versus non-sustainable projects is important. The way to make something sustainable is to engage people [so that they] want to keep coming back and follow through ... [The more] you're drawing people into taking ownership, the more real impact it'll have on their lives. [The] trick is really giving people the chance to engage with each other ... We introduce the Foldscope as a tool, but embed it in learning, continually planning for exit ... [We see this] as a whole toolbox for frugal science, so users anywhere can access parallel or similar capabilities to scientists and universities.'

Reducing waste through
teaching repair skills

THE
RESTART
PROJECT

+ 006ATK/RP/02

We are all familiar with keeping receipts for warranties or taking out 'extended warranty cover' on products we buy. However, rarely do we 'open up' those products if they go wrong, as we are terrified of invalidating those warranties. A group challenging this behaviour is the Restart Project, a social enterprise that helps people repair goods, reduce waste and re-establish a repair culture (006ATK/RP/01).

They run 'Restart Parties', free community events where experienced volunteers help others learn to repair and maintain broken objects (006ATK/RP/02). Broken items go through 'triage', with owners describing symptoms and volunteers offering diagnosis. Next, a volunteer and a participant try to repair the item together. The events focus on skill-sharing, with the enterprise now concentrating on helping other groups to replicate them. The intention is for people to take back control of their purchases, supporting the maker's mantra 'if you cannot open it, you do not own it'. In the following interview, co-founder Ugo Vallauri shared his insights.

'[The project] started from personal experiences; we had experience working in international development in Kenya, Mozambique, Brazil and East Timor, witnessing technology's role in bringing opportunities to people that weren't previously possible. Repair is a way to learn more about people's frustrations and interests in this area, so we keep running events to underpin this ... [Our] mission is to fix our relationship with electronics. We run repair events, where people share or learn skills, learning how to disassemble and reassemble all kinds of electronic products, delivered in ten countries. Our audience is everyone – whether you care for the environment, extending products' lives or empowering change through design or manufacture – because we are increasingly surrounded by electronics. Learning new skills is the overall agenda.' The biggest impact of their network has been 'working on 8,249 devices, successfully repairing 4,444, with 10,224 participants helped by 16,134 hours of volunteer time. We've prevented over 12.1 tonnes of waste going into landfill, and we've stopped 219,192 kilograms of CO_2 emissions, but that's just one layer. What's more exciting is learning how people find this path

to learn more, feeling empowered, providing opportunities to fight back, extending the life of products and giving back control.'

Vallauri cited the importance of community, holistic design approach and designing for material harvesting. 'I would recommend the events to anyone who is interested in designing future products, improving customer care, improving how we support products, how we develop better software - at a time when software support becomes possibly more crucial in extending the lifetime of products, compared to the way we just look at hardware.' He urged people to 'bring something you're struggling with, and see how the collective community support of Restart volunteers can [help you see] products differently. Also, interrogate the data ... and get involved ... [We] run a weekly podcast and radio show where we ask questions about the future of design, and how consumer rights should be interpreted in a different way, and how waste ultimately is just one part of this story.'

The Restart Project has 'conducted research with universities, highlighting the main barriers to people's ability to do this on their own. Partly, it's the lack of confidence, lack of access to information and a lack of access to tools and spare parts. Obviously, the lack of recognized, trustworthy commercial repair services, which actually is interesting because it highlights that, frequently, the problem is not just the way products are designed, but it's how the supporting services around products are often non-existent or very poor in comparison to the ease of access to brand-new products at a click of your mouse.' Vallauri said we must 'rethink the holistic approach to design, consume, reuse, remanufacture and, eventually, the end-of-life of products and electronics. We believe the skills of tomorrow are about problem-solving, being resourceful and resilient to surrounding ecosystems. One step is to find malfunctioning devices' faults and, potentially, spare parts, while gaining the most convenient and cost-effective access to components. It might involve worlds such as eBay, or [buying] multiple units, to ensure future part-harvesting. It brings into question how we source materials, how we give values to specific components that might have higher values than the whole artefact.'

+ 006ATK/LOT/01

Reducing waste through
social ownership

LIBRARY
OF
THINGS

+ 006ATK/LOT/02

Ever needed a drill, a barbecue, a tent or a sewing machine without borrowing from a mate? The Library of Things solves this problem of needing infrequently used things that are either financially out of reach or do not require permanent ownership. The Library of Things is a community space where people come to borrow useful items. The founders decided to build a test version in a space they found in a public library in West Norwood, South London (006ATK/LOT/01). The concept is simple: anyone can become a member, and it's free to join. The simple mechanism is based on volunteers and members. Volunteers who donate their time get unlimited free borrows complemented by learning new skills. Members can borrow up to five items a week. All the items are priced depending on their value and how much people want to borrow them.

Current offers include a bread-making machine for £4 per week, a barbecue for £5 and a garden hose for £1 (006ATK/LOT/02). The most popular items have been carpet cleaners and lawn mowers, with four-man tents and ukuleles close behind. The founders established the project via crowdfunding, and a local outlet of a DIY retailer donated stock, while outdoor brands Berghaus and Patagonia gave backpacks, travel duffle bags and other goods. The aspirations are far more radical; they are interested in how we can make organizations accountable to the community, and for members to be on a genuinely peer-to-peer level. It is very different from an Uber-style model, where sharing platforms are privately owned and operated. It is a non-profit company, with 500 members (more day by day) and three more outlets opening in 2018. Their primary goal is to make the scheme more sustainable. Future plans include launching a community share offer in order to allow the library to be owned by and accountable to its local community. In the pipeline they are working on a local delivery service, public supper club events, workshops for members, and boot camps to train others to set up their own libraries. Their audience includes low-income young professionals, young families, and civic and enterprise projects.

In an interview, co-founder Rebecca Trevalyan offered her insights. When asked about the project's impacts, she highlighted numerous examples, including a local mum: 'Mirela has been looking for suitable work since she took redundancy two years ago, and joined Library of Things as a volunteer. She talks about how much it means to her to be involved in her community and spend her time helping people. She is now making a small wage from the project, and is one of the Library's top borrowers. [She says] "I spent a day flying the Library's kite with my son Danny for the first time. At the end of the day he looked at me and said, Mum, this has been one of the best days of my life!"' Meanwhile, volunteer Oliver Kirkman says, 'One of my highlights has been helping a member and his daughter pick the things they wanted for her first camping trip. Another moment was seeing the kid-like grin on two grown men's faces as they walked out with the Nintendo 64.' The project shifts the barriers of product acquisition through ownership.

Trevalyan shared the teams' biggest insights. '[Operating] a shoestring version of Library of Things helped us learn so much about how people interacted with borrowing – and gave us the confidence to build a bigger version. People interact very differently with something they can see, hear and touch, than with a survey or concept. So our advice is [to] build the smallest version of your idea, then test it, change it, test it again – and keep going. The important thing too was giving a platform to hundreds of people to help shape the service, giving them a feeling of ownership. Down the line, this translates to hundreds of active advocates, crowdfunding backers and volunteers.' The Library of Things believes that by 'pioneering win-win models that make good business sense to people from many sectors' they can reach more sustainable models compared to NGOs for this type of work. For example, 'Library of Things is looking to lease items directly from corporate product manufacturers and lend those on to communities, meaning the corporates receive a financial return with every loan of their item. Housing Associations want to embed Library of Things into their developments because it brings social value to their tenants. Property developers want a Library of Things in new developments, partly because that makes it easier for them to sell smaller flats – and with the growing pressure on land in big cities, that makes a lot of sense.'

+ 007 COMMUNITY EN

007
COMMUNITY ENGAGEMENT

NITY
GAGE
MENT

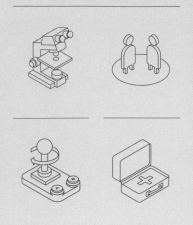

+ 007CE/CC/01

Building communities
through sharing
abundant goods

CASSEROLE CLUB

+ 007CE/CC/02

We are all familiar with wasted food – and an organization tackling this challenge is Casserole Club, a start-up working with individuals who aren't always able to cook for themselves. Club volunteers distribute extra portions of home-cooked food to local neighbours once a week, once a month or whenever works (007CE/CC/01). The project started with one person, a mobile phone and an Excel spreadsheet, acting on a hunch. Now, more than 7,000 people have signed up, with this number increasing daily.

The club knows from research, feedback and comments from organizations such as councils and housing associations that thousands of UK residents could benefit from the project. Working with local organizations and networks, its volunteers are increasing uptake and hopefully raising awareness of digital exclusion. One of the biggest challenges they have is ensuring people feel safe, protected and happy to participate. They have evolved the barrier to entry, ensuring it is not high and off-putting for cooks, while reassuring food consumers. In interview Matt Skinner, head of development, commented on their operation and wider lessons: '[Casserole Club] is a micro volunteering platform that connects people, specifically the elderly; often, they are socially isolated and vulnerable (007CE/CC/02). It is supported by quite lightweight technology, matching the cooks and diners based on interests and food preferences. We see the technology as the enabler of the friendship, rather than the thing they return to; our aim is to address the problem of social isolation.'

'[The club's core mission was tackling] malnutrition among older people, and was seen as a solution that could help them address adult social care costs, like Meals on Wheels services ... [After] almost four years, we would describe our core mission as tackling the root causes of social isolation among older people. We do this through food as a mechanism, joining and connecting people. We intended to help older people who are on the edges of receiving that kind of service. From a societal perspective it is the social contact and the relationship that is more important than the food itself ... [A perfect example of this] was a cook and diner in Surrey. The cook was sharing food on average once a week with a 95-year-old lady. We got a phone call from her, saying that, while she was dropping off a meal, the cook smelt strange odours and thought it was carbon monoxide; she got in touch with her boiler repair services and asked them to check it out and they condemned the boiler straight away.' This action saved the 95-year-old's life.

The organization was transparent about scaling challenges. '[The] people we are trying to find are socially isolated, and finding socially isolated people is not easy to do'; also, 'connecting a huge number of cooks who really want to take on Casserole Club themselves at a local level' is a challenge. Finally, they must overcome 'archaic systems around food hygiene standards, and criminal record checking'. They worked through these issues through collaborations and 'enabling people to show their ID online, rather than in person'.

The club puts the strongest lesson emphasis on models: 'The financial model, the operating model to scale the operation is something that needs addressing to undertake this type of work. There has been a lot of investment by technology projects, but the biggest value is time. The hard stuff is getting the business case, the finance and operating model. That is not as attractive to investors, but if you don't do those things, you get in trouble. We always think "behind the scenes", and anybody starting up needs to think about the processes and positives of it, to scale quickly. Being iterative with your business and operating models is super-important.'

'The club operates from FutureGov, a limited company, [but] thinking about sustainability from the get-go is critical ... we have been very lucky to get grants, but we have also been really conscious that those grants are not sustainable indefinitely. To bring in the money, we had to do the community organizing, running the service as a business as much as a social operation. We have been working on the skills and things that you need for this kind of work. We started with PR people and now we need to focus on being an entrepreneur, and doing the things that people find quite boring. Finally, partnership working is really essential.'

+ 007CE/SW/01

SOLIDWOOL

+ + We started a manufacturing company with a socially local vision, philosophy and strong ethics. I think if you have a set of ethics, a philosophy that you're working to, maybe it's what you say no to that really matters and helps shape you.

+ 007CE/SW/02

The founders of the Solidwool project witnessed the disappearance of their vibrant and productive local woollen industry. In recent years, coarse hill-farmed wool from upland sheep has dramatically dropped in value. Solidwool currently use wool from Herdwick sheep, an iconic breed from the British Lake District (007CE/SW/02). Traditionally used by the carpet industry, the Herdwick wool is now considered an almost worthless by-product of sheep farming, with the breeds' fleece being one of the lowest-value wools in the UK. The Herdwick is regarded as the most resilient of all British breeds, with up to 99% of them farmed in the Lake District. Currently a large mark-up is placed on the resale of wool, and this does not always translate to the farmer, so Solidwool seek to transform that balance. The result is Solidwool: a unique, composite material made from wool and biodegradable resin (007CE/SW/03). Their environmentally conscientious resin manufacturer claims a 33% reduction in carbon footprint and greenhouse gas emissions during manufacture over traditional resins. In interview founders Justin and Hannah Floyd share their insights into manufacturing to create value for local communities.

The project started as the founders 'wanted to stay local to Buckfastleigh in South Devon, an ancient woollen town. We felt strongly about ways, as designers, we could do good, have a positive impact by designing items requiring manufacture. At one point in time Buckfastleigh, or this whole area of South Devon, was the epicentre of the woollen industry in the UK. We're talking quite a long time ago, [as it's] now based around Yorkshire, but once this town had six mills making woollen cloth for the military, blankets, carpets and more. Now all that's left is the Devonia Sheepskins tannery. A lot of people leave to work elsewhere in South Devon or commute to Plymouth. We wanted to work with wool in Buckfastleigh,

+ 007CE/SW/03

+ 007CE/SW/04

+ + We use undervalued UK wool, which is typically from hill or mountain sheep and is really coarse and rough.

+ 007CE/SW/05

+ 007CE/SW/06

+ 007CE/SW/07

+ 007CE/SW/08

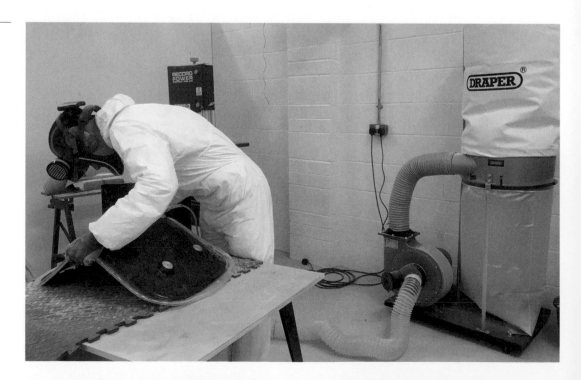

+ + Our mission is to bring wool-based manufacturing back to Buckfastleigh for a positive impact, using design to create skilled, interesting work for local people.

+ 007CE/SW/09

and bring wool-based manufacturing back to the town – through experimentation, lots of play, serendipity and wool industry peers commenting, "if your ambition is to use your skills, providing people with work, scale to the point you need to employ people". We decided on the use of wool as reinforcement in a composite material; we stumbled on this experiment while working in composites.

Their core mission is to bring wool-based manufacturing back to Buckfastleigh 'for positive impact, using design to create skilled, interesting work for local people ... [As] the project has developed, we very quickly realized there's a real impact with different wools we use. We use undervalued UK wool, typically from hill or mountain sheep, that is really coarse and rough. There's always an annual surplus and farmers get low returns for their crop. We can have a real impact on the financial return, as wool is the perfect renewable material. Whether or not you agree with farming sheep, every year there's this crop of fantastic material.'

'[After] three years in production (007CE/ SW/08), we will have more people employed, working alongside us. We're intending to have more direct purchasing with farmers. At the moment, farmers typically sell wool at auction; for Lake District Herdwick sheep, farmers get about 40p per kilogram. Currently I have to buy through wool merchants, paying roughly £2 a kilogram. That's washed wool, and 70p of that cost is washing. We believe that working directly with communities of farmers will improve the bottom line. If we don't change anything in the

price we purchase at, we return better value to the farmer ... [We started] a manufacturing company with a socially local vision, philosophy and strong ethics. I think if you have a set of ethics, a philosophy that you're working to, maybe it's what you say no to that really matters and helps shape you. I think the word "remarkable" is a word worth remembering, and helps [with] reflection and measuring of what you're doing. We have a unique material that is visual, with an irreplaceable set of values behind it, and it is remarkable. We could have thrown loads of money at this three years ago to make it easier for ourselves; because it's new technology, we would have done things differently to what we're doing now. That would have been a mistake, because it would have led us down the incorrect path. We've moved slowly, allowing us to learn and make mistakes with low risk. So, simplify as much as possible, because it makes the work you're doing easier, and it will make the external understanding of it clearer. People buy stories, not facts ... It's important and more honest, and more powerful, to communicate on a human level.'

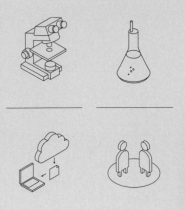

Designing experiences
that embed social
participation and
empathy

NEW
OLD
EXCHANGE

+ + Younger people were asking the sorts of questions you can't find answers to on Google, so we had a 15-year-old asking, 'What should I say at a funeral?'

+ 007CE/NOE/03

In Europe, half the population will be over 50 by 2020. Outside your family, for example, how many older people do you chat to? If you engaged more, would it evolve your perception of an 'ageing population'? In response to a Design Museum brief – 'Design a new product, service, system or experience to tackle ageing stigma and cut down prejudice' – Special Projects' designers created 'Exchange'. The 'living installation' gave exhibition visitors the opportunity to sit and talk to older people, and exchange experiences (007CE/NOE/01). Conversations were recorded on a custom-built 'giant notebook' table. The work was intended to tackle stigma and stereotypes against ageing, enabling visitors to experience design and research practices. The designers believed that 'human empathy is essential in creating compelling experiences'. It was so successful that celebrities Daphne Selfe and Lady Helen Hamlyn volunteered, and Quentin Blake drew for them. The installation was meticulously considered (007CE/NOE/03), creating an intimate environment. To provoke public responses, they created films that documented example queries from members of the public.

The following interview is with Adrian Westaway, Director of Technology and Magic at Special Projects. 'Our brief was "challenge stereotypes and stigma around ageing"; technology is central to everything we do, and our role as designers is to humanize that technology. We thought, "Let's try to share our process; instead of talking about technology, let's talk about people." We invited visitors to sit down and ask any question to a volunteer in their 70s or 80s. They were asked to write the question down on the table, keeping a handwritten record, and then spend 5 minutes discussing the answer. Only the question was recorded.' The space was carefully designed, surrounded by plants, making it human and comfortable for people. It was incredibly popular with people queuing to speak to the older adults. '[One] of the volunteers told me, "Nobody ever queues to speak to an old lady." In the context of the exhibition, the rest of the exhibits were very tech-focused; it was a strong reminder that people are who we design for ... [Some] members of the public came back every single day; some students used it as a research tool for projects on ageing.' A lot of the questions by the older adults were around being puzzled about technology, for example 'Why do you use your phone so much?' Interestingly, 'younger people were asking the sorts of questions that you can't find answers to on Google, e.g. "What should I say at a funeral?" They all relied on how you should behave, and a politeness. Things that are much harder to find

+ + The installation was incredibly popular, and people were queueing to speak to the older adults. One of the volunteers told the designers, 'Nobody ever queues to speak to an old lady.'

+ 007CE/NOE/04

in a more binary search, which was interesting because they were accessing the wisdom of their senior peers from a more social point of view. We had questions like, "Is it true that people don't grow up? When did you last make a sandcastle?" Lots of questions about happiness in life and "What should I do about jobs?" It was so good for us, as a studio, to have this constant contact with older adults. We ended up employing one of the volunteers; she comes to our studio once a month to talk to us, as a sort of contextual studio counselling service.'

Westaway said that, based on the content of that specific exhibition, 'there is a tendency now, looking at the products being designed, to minimize the human contact and replace that with some form of digital intervention. You look at all these gadgets, chatbots and AI conversational interfaces, but at the end of the day we're working with a human who has needs and emotions … It was just a reminder that while some of these technologies are very impressive because they're so new, we have a very, long way to go if we want to replace human contact. It was a very strong reminder to respect human contact … Involving real people in an exhibition is compelling and was a fantastic way of benchmarking the other items on show. Designers can always benefit from surrounding

themselves in the reality and context in which their creations will be used. Too often, concept videos and advertisements offer a completely false view of how the product will interact with its users. Our exhibit was located right next to the Paro robotic seal, and just having an 86-year-old woman next to a robot that's been designed to replace her carer offered the most striking reality check on whether these products are the best solution for the ageing population.'

THE
BEVY

Providing social glue,
accessible to all

+ 007CE/TB/01

+ + The trick for funders and charitable foundations is supporting people in true need that struggle with paperwork. We want to be a blueprint for pubs in the future.

+ 007CE/TB/02

Pubs are central to some communities, as they level people socially, and help build community support and companionship. Historically, Moulsecoomb near Brighton has been plagued by crime and unemployment. The Bevy seeks to buck that trend, providing community-run amenities. Anyone can become a shareholder for £10. They own a wheelchair-accessible 'Bevy Bus' (007CE/TB/01) to collect residents for community clubs, bring their sponsored rugby team back after games and take local Albion football fans to every home game. The initiative helps young people gain work experience, a prerequisite for modern employment. They also host plant sales there, provide fruit and veg to their lunch club and make puddings, jams and pickles, raising funds for their community Christmas events.

They have partnered with local St John's College, bringing students to work in the kitchen, delivering meals and building skills. The pub works with the local council's learning disability employment team to offer short work placements behind the bar. Volunteers mow lawns, fix the drains, collect glasses (when busy), do a bar stint, organize events and tackle business paperwork. The Bevy also runs budgeting workshops, and hosts health checks and monthly councillor drop-in surgeries,

as well as sponsoring a student rugby team who, in exchange, do some volunteering. They are working with local breweries to launch their own beer, leading to more employment and sustained revenue (007CE/TB/02). In the following interview co-founder Warren Carter shared their accrued knowledge.

'[The Bevy pub was] closed by authorities, [and] remained shut for years. Locals felt Moulsecoomb and Bevendean Estates were isolated, as the location was in the country's bottom 5% for deprivation. We looked at community pubs, realizing we were the UK's first "housing estate pub". We knew, if we reopened to keep it commercially viable, we had to be more than a pub ... [Pubs] are in our DNA; if run properly, they include anyone ... [The Bevy] needed to be like your front room, with activities and a place to meet. An old-fashioned pub where people knew everyone, with good service, [that] was affordable – but the mission was always a back-to-front community centre, with countless activities to benefit the neighbourhood.'

'[The Bevy had] a bad reputation, and was seen as an unviable pub. The first email I got was from a local copper, saying "There's no chance we're going to let you reopen this pub", leading

+ 230

+ FUTUREKIND
+ 007 COMMUNITY ENGAGEMENT

+ THE BEVY

OPPOSITE:
+ 007CE/TB/04

+ + The first email I got was from a local copper, saying 'There's no chance we're going to let you reopen this pub.'

+ 007CE/TB/03

to perception issues. We were in a unique position, so it's been a struggle financially. We don't own the building, so we're not getting rent from flats upstairs, so it's standalone, in an area with lots of poverty.' Their ethos reflects the fact that 'it's a pub, a community centre, and we want to be there for everyone within the neighbourhood. Since forming, we run clubs, choirs, Friday Friends disability groups (007CE/TB/03), cooking in the kitchen, a training kitchen for children, pigeon clubs and normal things you'd find in a pub. If someone comes up with an idea, we try and make it happen; it's good for The Bevy, good for the business and it really gets people engaged.'

One of their biggest successes is their Friday Friends seniors' club, 'helping up to 40 older residents a week. They get picked up by minibus, have lunch, a laugh and a bit of bingo. It tackles loneliness head on, giving people the chance to get out of their four walls, encouraging conversation and community. Some of our work with disabled people has been amazingly impactful. It's still a working-class pub, with numerous builders finishing work and having a drink. St John's College for young adults with learning disabilities run a kitchen two or three times a week, and we offer work experience behind the bar. We want to build opportunities for people with disabilities, who are never given chances to work. We can't afford chefs, because we don't make enough money from the food. So, we married the two, the work experience, so people can get a stepping stone to proper jobs and paid work.'

'[The] pub wouldn't survive without volunteers; if you walked into Wetherspoon's and they said, "Oh, we're busy, can you clear the glasses?" or "We've run out of loo roll, can you pop to the shops?" you'd tell them where to go ... [They] want to be everyone's pub, while making savings – because, commercially, we're an unviable pub, socially we're massively viable ... [The] trick for funders and charitable foundations is supporting people in true need that struggle with paperwork. We want to be a blueprint for pubs in the future (007CE/TB/04). It's hard work, you must be bloody-minded, and people need to visit parallel projects, learning from them.'

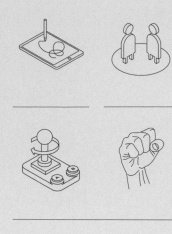

+ 007CE/F/01

Empowering
communities
through fixing

FIXPERTS

+ 007CE/F/02

Fixperts is a social-design project that shares knowledge through an online platform. The non-profit was established to motivate and equip people to get more hands-on with the world around them. They believe that 'fixing is a valuable creative and social resource'. Through their creative platform and education project, they invite people to build their skills in making and repair by fixing things for others, and to create content that encourages others to do the same. Originally founded by the designers Daniel Charny and James Carrigan, Fixperts is now part of the 'think and do tank' FixEd, which is focused on education, developing courses with universities and schools, workshops for children, and business-partner consultancy.

A Fixperts project runs to a simple template. Teams include designers or makers and storytellers, who capture the process and make mini documentaries. The teams work directly with a Fix Partner, who is a real person with something they need to fix. Fixperts believe that, through small fixes, they can 'give people the insight and confidence to find solutions for themselves and others'. All Fixperts teaching materials and an archive of 500 Fix Films are available online to encourage social design. The Tavistock Institute recently analysed the social initiative, identifying stakeholder impacts: 'For students it developed technical design and transferable skills; for the Fix Partners there was an opportunity to work with designers to build useful products [solving] real problems; for the educational institutions it was a vehicle for teaching social design.'

The educational potential of the project was unforeseen, but its use in universities and schools has become the main success story. Fixperts' mission is now to 'support the next generation of designers, engineers and makers to be creative problem-solvers'. When asked about lessons learned, Charny responded, 'First, is that we have had to really watch and listen. Understanding how we're being used and who our real audience is has been key for us, and it has changed through time. Like many social projects, we have very limited resources against a really big agenda. Fixperts was very wide at the beginning. We started under a sustainability umbrella, we've done a range of work around ageing, disability and inclusive design, and we've been used as a framework for invention and innovation. We're all of these things still, but we have to be very clear about focusing on where we're most relevant – in education. We may evolve further; to some degree, we're in perpetual pilot mode. That's one thing. The other is to do with making the most of the context and connections that we've had, and being as opportunistic as possible. We try not to spend a lot of time trying to raise grants and sponsorship; it's really hard work, and often you end up losing sight of the real goal. We'd prefer to work smart and focus on the activities that get us the most impact.'

'[So it's] about getting things going and prototyping in the most local, immediate [way] ... Of course, think about the bigger picture – answer the question about what you're a part of – but try to test the feasibility and prove your impact immediately. This will help move your project from "nice to have" to "essential". Social design, social benefit, should be driving our profession. I'd like to see designers removing barriers; that's not a "nice" thought; it can also be a commercial imperative. Design being used to remove barriers means more people can access goods and services. You widen markets and create new ones; you respond to a changing world. For our part, our interest is changing design cultures, which is why we shifted our focus from individual designers, makers and engineers to people that teach design. Fixperts is now almost entirely an education programme, with a focus on disseminating guidelines to tutors and teachers, and supporting the film archive, which has become a central teaching resource as well as a great way to inspire wider audiences. We've moved from working at the undergrad and postgrad level to working with younger children, and we've found that Fixperts is well suited as a framework for STEM [science, technology, engineering and mathematics], STEAM [science, technology, engineering, the arts and mathematics] and D&T [design and technology]. In 2016 we co-produced a draft for a new technical STEM award at GCSE level in England, and that was a really satisfying moment.' At the time of writing, Fixperts has been taught in 20 countries, and in more than 40 higher-education institutes.

This book is dedicated to my family: Serena, Molly and Bryn, with the support of our Lewes 'relatives'... in all their forms. Thank you to the Design Products department at the Royal College of Art, for helping to identify relevant areas of interest, and to the dean of design, Professor Paul Anderson, for his support. Specific thanks go to James Tooze, a great strategist, who is responsible for the taxonomic illustrations. Lastly, a special mention to Professor Sharon Baurley, a colleague at the RCA, and to my lifelong mentor, Professor Roberto Fraquelli of Schumacher College, Devon, which is rethinking approaches to sustainability.

Of course, none of this would have been possible without the help and cooperation of the featured projects: 30 Dollar Wind Turbine, Ambionics, AzuKo, Better Shelter, Casserole Club, ColaLife, Diva Centres, Eco Wave Power, Elephant Listening Project, FairCap, FairPhone, Farm Hack, FarmBot, Field Ready, FixMyStreet, Fixperts, Foldscope, Folia Water, Future Sense, GravityLight, Hiut Denim, Kniterate, Land Life, Library of Things, Litterati, MakeHealth, MamaOpe Jacket, Motivation, New Ground Housing, New Old Exchange, Ode, On Our Radar, Open Toilets, Open Water Project, Opendesk, OpenStructures, People's Fridge, PET Lamp, PlayPump, Precious Plastics, Public Lab, Safecast, SafePoint, Showerloop, Simprints, Smart Citizen, Smart Hydro Power, Solar Stove, Solidwool, Sugru, TechforTrade, The Bevy, The Plastic Tide, The Restart Project, Vertical University, Virtual Doctors, WikiHouse and WonderSphere. Thank you for your time, and for bringing 'Futurekind' one step closer.

Cover and prelims

Cover, front Clockwise from top left: 3D-printed ceramic water filter. Design by Unfold. Photo: OS_Studio; © David Constantine – Motivation; courtesy of TechforTrade; Wonder Connection's WonderSphere, designed by Bresslergroup. Photo: Steve Belkowitz; courtesy of Sugru; courtesy of Simprints; courtesy of Rodd; courtesy of Opendesk

Cover, back Anti-clockwise from top left: © Studio Alvaro Catalán de Ocón; courtesy of Future Sense; Public Lab contributors and Gowanus Low Altitude Mapping, licensed under CC-BY-SA; courtesy of MakeHealth; Tim Wille; © Studio Alvaro Catalán de Ocón; Turjoy Chowdhury; courtesy of One Earth Designs; courtesy of Ambionics

1 Clockwise from top left: courtesy of FarmBot; 3D-printed ceramic water filter. Design by Unfold. Photo: OS_Studio; courtesy of FixMyStreet, licensed under CC BY 4.0; courtesy of Smart Citizen; courtesy of FairPhone; courtesy of Opendesk; © 2019 FairCap CIC; courtesy of Solidwool; courtesy of FarmBot
2 Tim Wille
6 © Studio Alvaro Catalán de Ocón

Civic Empowerment

16–21 Courtesy of Future Sense
22 mySociety, licensed under CC BY 4.0
23 Mark Longair, licensed under CC BY 4.0
24–27 Courtesy of One Earth Designs
28–31 Courtesy TechforTrade
32–35 Courtesy On Our Radar
36 Courtesy of Better Shelter. Photo: Erik Hagman
37t Courtesy of UNHCR. Photo: Sebastian Rich
37b Courtesy of Better Shelter
38 Courtesy of UNHCR Photo: Jiro Ose
39t Courtesy of UNHCR. Photo: Sebastian Rich
39b Courtesy of Better Shelter. Photo: Jonas Nyström
40 Ross Atkins
41t Jo-Anne Bichard
41b Jo-Anne Bichard
42–45 Courtesy of Litterati
46 Public Lab contributors, licensed under CC-BY-SA
47 Public Lab contributors and Gowanus Low Altitude Mapping, licensed under CC-BY-SA
48 The Craft Market, Maria Lamadrid, Public Lab contributors, licensed under CC-BY-SA
49 Public Lab contributors, licensed under CC-BY-SA
50 Public Lab contributors, licensed under CC-BY-SA
51 Public Lab contributors, NOLA Green Team, licensed under CC-BY-SA
52–53 Courtesy of People's Fridge
54–55 Courtesy of Pollard Thomas Edwards

Health

60–63 Courtesy of ColaLife
64–65 Courtesy of MamaOpe
66–69 Courtesy of SafePoint

70–73 © 2019 FairCap CIC
74–77 Courtesy of Rodd
78–79 Theresa Dankovich
80–83 Courtesy of MakeHealth
84–85 Courtesy of Virtual Doctors
86–89 Courtesy of IDEO.org

Environment + Sustainability

92–95 Courtesy of FarmBot
96–101 Courtesy of FairPhone
102–05 Courtesy of Jason Selvarajan/Showerloop
106–07 Courtesy of Smart Hydro Power
108–13 Courtesy of Deciwatt Ltd
114–15 Courtesy of Vertical University
116–19 Courtesy of Land Life
120–21 Courtesy of Daniel Connell
122–23 Courtesy of Eco Wave Power
124–27 Courtesy of Eleanor L. H. Mackay/The Plastic Tide
128–29 Courtesy of Farm Hack

Accessible Design

132–33 Photos: Kniterate
134–37 Courtesy of Sugru
138–39 Courtesy of Ambionics
140–45 Courtesy of WikiHouse
146 OS WaterBoiler. Design by Jesse Howard. Photo: Jesse Howard
147 OS CoffeeGrinder. Design by Unfold. Photo: Kristof Vrancken
148 Transparent kitchen tools. Design by Jesse Howard. Graphic: Jesse Howard
149t Transparent kitchen tools. Design by Jesse Howard. Graphic: Jesse Howard
149b OS WaterBoiler. Design by Jesse Howard. Photo: Jesse Howard
150–51 Courtesy of Safecast
152–55 Courtesy of Precious Plastics
156–57 Courtesy of Field Ready

158 Courtesy of Open Water Project
159t Courtesy of Open Water Project
159b Courtesy of Open Water Project. Illustrations by Akshaya Sawant

Economic Empowerment

162–69 © Studio Alvaro Catalán de Ocón
170–71 Courtesy PlayPumps, www.playpumps.co.za
172 © David Constantine: Motivation
173 © David Constantine: Motivation
174–75 © David Constantine: Motivation
176 © Matt Grayson
177 © David Constantine: Motivation
178–79 Courtesy of Hiut Denim
180–85 Courtesy of Simprints
186–91 Turjoy Chowdhury
192–97 Courtesy of Opendesk

Access to Knowledge

200–01 Wonder Connection's WonderSphere, designed by Bresslergroup. Photos: Steve Belkowitz
202 Peter Wrege
203 Andrea Turkalo
204 Liz Rowland
205 Ana Verahrami
206–07 Courtesy of Smart Citizen
208–09 Courtesy of Foldscope
210 Photo by Brendan Foster for The Restart Project
211 Photo by Heather Agyepong for The Restart Project
212 Courtesy of Library of Things

Community Engagement

216–17 Courtesy of Casserole Club
218 Joe Watson Photography
219 Jim Marsden Photography
220 Jim Marsden Photography
221 Jim Marsden Photography
222–23 Courtesy of Solidwool
224–27 Special Projects, press@specialprojects.studio
228–31 Courtesy of The Bevy
232 Kyoto Institute of Technology, KYOTO Design Lab
233 Sophie Both and Dan Jackson at Kingston University